MODERN CHRISTIAN MOVEMENTS

MODERN
CHRISTIAN
MOVEMENTS

John T. McNeill

Philadelphia

THE WESTMINSTER PRESS

Library of Congress Catalogue Card No.: 54-8839

PRINTED IN THE UNITED STATES OF AMERICA

CONTENTS

PREFACE

The substance of these chapters, with the exception of numbers 4 and 5, was presented in Queen's Theological College, Kingston, Ontario, in October, 1950, on the Chancellor's Lectureship founded by Sir Sanford Fleming. I owe a special debt of gratitude to the Board of the college, and to the professors and alumni, whose invitation gave the impulse to begin the book and who during the lectures constituted a keen and stimulating audience. All six of the topics have since been discussed in lectures at various ministers' schools held under the auspices of Union Theological Seminary, Auburn Seminary, and the General Board of Education of the Methodist Church. Conversations with many who were in attendance at these meetings has convinced me that there exists an extraordinary vagueness, coupled with curiosity, concerning the movements here described, among persons otherwise religiously informed. I am convinced too that a fuller knowledge of these key movements of modern Church history would help greatly toward an understanding of the present-day condition and prospects of Christianity, and prove stimulating to the religious life of both ministers and laymen.

JOHN T. McNEILL

Elmsdale, East Middlebury, Vermont
New Year's Day, 1954

INTRODUCTION

Most readers of this book will find in it descriptions of their own religious heritage. They are in some measure the heirs of the important movements, here described, that have stirred Western Christianity during the eventful centuries from the seventeenth to the twentieth. Historians of literature, philosophy, and science frequently refer to the seventeenth century as introducing the modern era. That century saw the chief works of Shakespeare and of Cervantes, the entire production of Milton and of Molière, the vastly influential philosophies of Bacon, Descartes, and Spinoza, the epochal forward thrust of science in the discoveries of Kepler, Galileo, and Newton. These are eminent names among the pioneers of the modern world. It was in their century too that the principles of representative and responsible government that have since prevailed and are today defended were first persistently advocated by many writers and fervently adopted by considerable numbers of mankind.

For the history of Christianity that period was hardly less significant. By 1600 the Reformation as a general movement had spent its force. The national and territorial Churches that had been shaped by it were now to be shaken and divided, both by the impact of political forces and by internal movements whose beginners were intent upon further reform. Nowhere was the conflict more intense or more vividly religious than in England, where the aggregation of forces that we call Puritanism gained a temporary ascendancy. Puritanism proved both divisive and creative. Revolting from the Anglican "Settlement," its spirit produced an unsettlement, a habitual religious discontent with the state of things. As in no previous age, this has become a constant element of the modern climate, manifesting itself both in an anxious and querulous perfectionism and in a healthy urge for reform. It was characteristic of the Puritan that he viewed the world of men as under the judgment of God; only rarely did he mistake his own judgment for the divine — with devastating results. In so far as we think of social justice as a concern of God, we are following in the way of the Puritans, and are not improbably acting under their influence. Puritanism has left a legacy of great importance not only to England but to the world.

Slightly later in the date of its flowering, but hardly less influential, was German Pietism, a reforming reaction to complacent Lutheranism. That most dismal conflict the Thirty Years' War had left Germany materially exhausted and spiritually enfeebled. Pietism wrought a revival, giving to German Protestantism new devotional reality and social power and sending forth its leaven into all the West and ultimately into all the world. Few people today have any realization of the historic importance of Pietism, or of its contribution to the religious life of later times.

The resemblances and differences of these two related movements will come to the reader's attention in the chapters that follow. Taken together, and in all their aspects, they comprise most of the significant phenomena of Protestantism between 1603, when James I came to the English throne, and 1740, when Frederick the Great of Prussia began his reign with favors to the opponents of Pietism. At its origin, Pietism was somewhat indebted to Puritanism. The two movements remained distinct, but were never arrayed against each other. They contributed jointly and harmoniously to the formation and nourishment of later movements. Methodism drew not a little of its austerity from the one; from the other, much of its ardor. Calvinist Evangelicals too were indebted to Puritanism and in a less degree to Pietism. The revivals that largely recruited the membership of American frontier Churches owed something to both. Certain leaders of both movements — the names of Baxter and Zinzendorf come at once to mind — were prominent advocates of Christian unity in times not so hospitable to such views as our own.

The world mission of nineteenth century Protestantism was foreshadowed by the work of men like the Cambridge Puritan John Eliot and the Halle Pietist Bartholomew Ziegenbalg. Every active member of a present-day Protestant communion is well aware of the missionary and ecumenical interests of his Church; he may not be aware how much of this concern is derived from the attitudes and achievements of resourceful Puritans and Pietists who charted and began tasks not yet completed. So far at least as religion is concerned, we can rightly comprehend our own beliefs and circumstances only in the perspective of history.

In that perspective too the intense struggles and controversies of the modern centuries yield their lessons. Controversy tends to shut us off from our opponents as by an iron curtain. It is left to a later generation to see in the light of history how much has been lost because of these barriers — and how much overt or clandestine trade across them has been carried on. While we repudiate one another's viewpoints, we silently interchange spiritual goods. The Oxford Movement of the 1830's was extremely shocking to typical Protestantism, not only because it deplored the Reformation but because it advocated practices in worship that had long been denounced as superstitious and feared as tokens of the revival of Romanism. Today the prevailing Protestant attitude is somewhat different from this. It is relatively tolerant of Anglo-Catholicism, and even grateful to it for some things. No longer are all medieval features of worship indiscriminately condemned as unscriptural perversions. Informed Protestants have come to realize that the Reformation itself retained numerous traditional church practices, including forms of private confession. They may prefer a relatively simple common worship and remain unimpressed by high doctrines of apostolic succession in the episcopate. But they are generally prepared to respect the convictions of those to whom these are important, and to profit by the products of their devotional life. It is apparent that Anglo-Catholicism, despite its alienation from Protestantism, has already shed something of its influence over most of the Protestant Churches. The fact that there is growing within them a recognition of the significance of the Church, one, catholic, and holy, as a living element of belief is in part a consequence of the impact of this movement. Yet it would be reckless to ascribe this result solely to this cause. Because the Oxford Tractarians were the earliest vigorous modern exponents of a doctrine of the divine role of the Church, it is difficult for their successors to realize that the sixteenth century Reformers were equally convinced of this. Modern Protestantism had forgotten the High-churchmanship of John Calvin. John Williamson Nevin of the " Mercersburg School " called attention to it in the 1840's when the Oxford Movement was still young. The Protestant revival of churchmanship now in progress assumes a conception of the Church nearer to that of the Reformed theologians than to that of Pusey and Keble. Yet the emphasis laid upon this element of theology by the Oxford men and their later disciples has undoubtedly stimulated the Protestant mind. Definitions of the Church Catholic may remain divergent while devotion to it becomes a common experience.

The modern history of Roman Catholicism is of incalculable importance, and replete with lessons for Christians beyond its ranks. Having become in the sixteenth century a dismayed remnant left behind by the Reformation, it made a valiant recovery of morale largely through the heroism and assiduity of the Jesuits. But its political claims were flouted in the Peace of Westphalia (1648) and its territories extinguished with the unification of Italy (1870). It was sometimes, as in the Jansenist controversy, torn by bitter internal strife, and it was subjected to humiliation by France, Austria, and other nations in which it had enjoyed a privileged status. It declared new dogmas such as the immaculate conception, papal infallibility, and the assumption of Mary, in defiance of modern intellectual liberalism. But after reaching a low point in political significance and affirming some of the most unmodern principles, it entered upon a rising curve of influence. Since the accession of Pope Leo XIII in 1878 it has made rapid gains in the prevailingly Protestant nations and become a pervasive force in American life. Among the factors that have made this possible are a tenacious adherence to claims of unique divine authority, the powerful leadership of able popes, the devotion of an alert priesthood to the advancement of their Church, and attention to the training of the laity. In areas where

Roman Catholicism has continually enjoyed unrivaled strength and influence, however, its condition is less vigorous. Through its sense of history and unfailing memory of historic experiences, its organization has become extraordinarily adaptable in unessential matters, sensitive to changes of environment and capable of meeting emergencies. It has also commanded the allegiance of many devout souls whose religious insights are highly valuable to all who care to profit by them.

It is altogether a wholesome thing for us who are outside the Roman Catholic Church to cultivate toward it a spirit of fair inquiry. If we remain strangers to its thought and to the movements that have stirred within it since our ancestors severed communion with it long ago, it will be to us a baffling enigma, and if we shun the company of its saints, we shall miss a great stimulation. Many an old-time Puritan was a reader of the thirteenth century Scholastics; many a Pietist and Evangelical fed upon the *Imitation of Christ,* the *Letters* of Fénelon, or the *Thoughts* of Pascal, and familiarized himself with the decrees of the Council of Trent. Like all things else on earth, the Roman Church is subject to change, and Protestants are apt to look upon it as if it had not changed. Yet its changes are mainly adaptations to environment without conscious infringement of traditional principles. Perhaps its modern history offers the most remarkable example that could be cited of the co-ordination of stable purpose with adaptability. Some elements of a useful knowledge of these matters will be found in our closing chapter.

Most of us have an interest in tracing our family genealogies. There are ancestries and posterities, too, in the movements that have deeply affected mankind. It is, of course, rarely if ever possible to say that a movement of thought or religion is born simply of two parent movements, but something analogous to parentage can often be established. Not only do the same genes run through Puritanism, Pietism, and Evangelicalism, but the whole series of fresh awakenings in the modern history of Christianity, however divergent in purpose, bear a family resemblance. They share the cultural atmosphere common to the period from the Puritan to the atomic age. It is unfortunate that the great majority of Christians are content with a fragmentary and unsure knowledge of the Christian past. So far as the post-Reformation period is concerned, the Church historians have themselves been at fault. How many of the most eminent scholars have broken off the story four centuries — or even fourteen centuries — ago! It is a commonplace in the Church history fraternity that we have no good history, either scholarly or popular, of Christianity in the modern era. Not even such a book as this one has appeared, employing illustrations from typical sources to exhibit briefly the principal Western Christian movements since the Reformation and to show the links that connect them.

There is abroad a growing conviction that now, at least so far as external conditions are concerned, a new and distinct era has begun. It was announced by a dazzling flash of light over the desert near Alamogordo at the dawn of a July morning in 1945. The scientific mastery of power has become potentially complete. The initial astonishment has tended to yield to settled fear; but it would be a foolish pessimism to conclude that the new age will be characterized principally by dread of the destructive devices of science. It is, however, certain to be a time of rapid change, many perils, and much perplexity.

Religion seems to be making a fresh appeal to our perplexed generation. Men may be fascinated by science and technology, but these of themselves cannot reach the height of man's requirements. The human body may travel faster than the speed of sound, but it does not leave the soul behind. Nor does its motion match the lightning flash of thought that can overleap in a moment hemispheres and epochs, or, as Milton wrote, " wander through eternity." Not less, but rather more, because a new orientation is demanded of us do we need to fortify ourselves with whatever spiritual assets we may bring out of the past. This book is an attempt to make more available some of the stored-up riches of the modern centuries for people fated to hear, or journey in, jet planes, apprehensive of atomic devastation, or impatiently awaiting the application of unlimited power to every physically difficult task. Man's essential needs remain, and they include the Godward orientation of his soul in freedom.

ENGLISH PURITANISM

I

The character of Malvolio in *Twelfth Night* has left Shakespearean critics engaged in a gentlemanly debate over the interesting question, Is Malvolio a Puritan, and does Shakespeare in portraying this unamiable character express his antipathy to Puritanism? Shakespeare may indeed have been quite conscious that he was giving his readers something to argue about. " Sometimes," says Maria, " he is a kind of puritan," and a few lines later, " The devil a puritan that he is, or anything constantly, but a time-pleaser; an affection'd ass." Now Shakespeare, using the phrase " a kind of puritan " in 1601, was doubtless aware that Puritans were not all of one kind. The name " Puritan " was often, in Shakespeare's age and later, applied rather indiscriminately, and this indefiniteness has persisted in modern discussion. The word has had a wide popular use for a person who follows a strict habit of life. *A Discourse Concerning Puritans* (1641), an anonymous tract attributed to Henry Parker but also to John Ley, indicates the way in which it was employed by some who scoffed at Puritanic scruples:

" In the mouth of a drunkard, he is a Puritan which refuseth his cups: in the mouth of a swearer he which feares an oath; in the mouth of a libertine, he which makes any scruple of common sin: in the mouth of a rude souldier, he which wisheth the Scottish War to an end without blood."

Richard Baxter, who was born in 1615, remembered how his father, who had no objections to the Prayer Book, was called Puritan, precisian, and hypocrite because he avoided popular amusements, read the Scriptures, prayed in his household, and reproved the drunken and profane.

But in church circles, the Puritans were primarily protesters on behalf of a more sweeping reform, particularly with reference to worship and ceremonial, than Anglicanism afforded. A letter of Thomas Sampson to Peter Martyr, of January, 1560, gives clear expression to one Puritan's distress over these matters at the moment when the Elizabethan settlement of religion was being shaped:

" Oh, my father, what can I hope for when the ministry of the Word is banished from court? while the crucifix is allowed with lights burning before it? . . . What can I hope, when three of our lately appointed bishops are to officiate at the Table of the Lord, one as priest, another as deacon, and a third as subdeacon, before the image of the crucifix, or at least not far from it, with candles, and habited in the golden vestments of the papacy? . . . What hope is there of any good when our party are disposed to look for religion in these dumb remnants of idolatry and not from the preaching of the lively Word of God? . . . I will propose this single question for your resolution . . . whether the image of the crucifix, placed on the Table of the Lord with lighted candles, is to be regarded as a thing indifferent; and if it is not to be considered so, but as an unlawful and wicked practice, then I ask, suppose the queen should enjoin all the bishops and clergy either to admit this image together with the candles into their churches or to retire from the ministry of the Word, what should be our conduct in this case? "

This was the great case of conscience for Puritans in holy orders. Four years later Sampson, along with Lawrence Humphrey, in an address to Archbishop Parker said:

" Conscience is a tender thing, and all men cannot look upon the same things as indifferent. If therefore these habits seem so to you, you are not to be condemned by us. On the other hand, if they do not appear so to us, we ought not to be vexed by you."

Robert Crowley in *A Brief Discourse Against the Outward Apparell and Ministring Garmentes of the Popische Church* (1566), writing of things not commanded or forbidden in Scripture, shows us how conscience must sometimes decide where Scripture is silent:

"We graunt that of themselves they be things indifferent . . . but
when the use of them will destroy or not edifie, then ceasse they to be
so indifferent that in such case we may use them."

Certainly these ecclesiastical habiliments were not the concern of
Malvolio, Shakespeare's spoilsport who would have no cakes and
ale. There were some very religious Puritans too whose interests
lay elsewhere. This is true of William Perkins of Cambridge, whom
Louis B. Wright has dubbed "Elizabethan apostle of practical divinity." In 1642, just forty years after Perkins' death, Thomas Fuller
said of him: "An excellent Chirurgeon [surgeon] he was at the
joynting of a broken soul and at stating of a doubtful conscience."
It was as a guide of conscience that he was most celebrated; but he
was also held in high esteem as a theologian and as a defender of the
doctrine of predestination, to which, at that time, most Anglicans
as well as Puritans firmly adhered. Perkins knows well, too, that
conscience is a tender thing — perhaps we ought to say in his case,
a terrifying thing. He once wrote:

"Let a man commit any trespass or offense, though it be done in
secret and concealed from the knowledge of any person living, yet conscience does know of it and will accuse him and terrify him, cite him
before God, and give him no rest."

Perkins, however, treated conscience in relation to other problems
than those which exercised Sampson.

Most Puritan diaries are replete with evidence of the haunting
specter of an accusing conscience. This is how it affects Richard
Rogers, a student of Perkins (1589):

"So many thoughtes stuffe my minde. . . . But the chiefest is mine
evel heart which cannot setle to study. . . . Oh Lord, what heavenly
bookes lye by me unoccupied and unsearched."

And here is John Ward lamenting his sins (1595):

"My incontinent thoughts at Hobson's . . . my great mirth at bowling
after supper . . . my immoderate eating of wallnutes and cheese after
supper whereby I did distemper my body . . . [And equally to the

point]: My confused lecture which I red to my auditores . . . my want
of meditation with Christ when I ly down to sleep. My drowsines in
reading Ursinus . . . also my intemperate eating of damzens."

The sins that worried many Puritans were their own, but many
of them too were primarily concerned with the sins of others. Some
prominent Puritans spent their energies in animated controversy
over the polity and ministry of the Church. They cried out against
prelacy as unscriptural, and they defended as Scriptural a Presbyterian or an Independent model of church government. There were
still others who explored the depths and heights of spiritual and
mystical experience.

It is obvious then, at the outset, that the term Puritanism is a
comprehensive one, a blanket thrown over a wide variety of critics
and moralists. Puritanism had no founder. Carlyle's famous statement that John Knox was " high priest and founder " of Puritanism
is rhetorically good and historically bad. Knox was only one of those
who contributed to its early development, and very many who must
be embraced in the category of Puritans would have contended
against him to the uttermost. Indeed, to describe Puritanism as a
" movement " is to suggest too much of unity and purpose. It has
something of the variety, color, and motion of a Brueghel canvas.

Historians have used the word " Puritanism " so comprehensively
as to include those of all groups who objected to the worship or
polity of the Anglican Church, and stood, so to speak, on the Protestant side of Anglicanism in its relations with Rome. It is difficult
to define very accurately a term that is made to apply alike to the
Separatist Robert Brown and the Presbyterian Thomas Cartwright;
to men like William Perkins and Thomas Adams, Puritan voices
within Anglicanism; to John Smyth, William Ames, John Robinson, and the rest of the variant band who went into exile; to the
Smectymnuans, along with the Five Dissenting Brethren. The term
becomes still more miscellaneous in its application when we include
the Quakers, Seekers, Ranters, Fifth Monarchy Men, Family of
Love, Levellers, Diggers, and Muggletonians; restless propagandists
like William Prynne; mystics like Peter Sterry and Sir Francis Rous;

individuals so different as Richard Baxter, John Bunyan, and George
Fox; or the amazing New Englanders, Roger Williams, with his
bold program of toleration, and the introspective Cotton Mather,
now prone on his study floor humiliated by his sins, and again writing in his diary (February 9, 1684):

"In passing along the streets, I have set myself to bless thousands of
persons who never knew I did it, with secret wishes after this manner
sent unto heaven for them."

The fact is that a recklessly extensive application of the word
"Puritan" has become habitual and virtually unavoidable. The discriminating student will seek to set the variant forms of Puritanism
in logical categories. He may, for example, classify the Puritans as
conforming Puritans, Presbyterians, Separatists and Independents,
spiritual sectarians and miscellaneous fanatics. (In somebody's eyes
all of us are sectarians and many of us fanatics.) But when we have
catalogued them in this or any other convenient way, and have
given our attention to the peculiarities of those in each class, we shall
hardly excuse ourselves from the attempt to view Puritanism as a
whole. We shall then recognize, I believe, that, with the possible
exception of some of the wilder (and smaller) sects, all these varieties
have something in common.

We may sense this common element and yet find it very difficult
to identify and describe. Let us reflect on the word "Puritanism"
and its connotations. It so happens that the term, though offensive
to those to whom it was applied, was not ineptly chosen. Though
its use has been incautiously extended, the groups and persons com-
prehended under it were all intent upon purifying the Church, as
they understood matters, from accumulated corruptions and abuses
which official Anglicanism seemed content to retain. All that was
nonscriptural in polity, worship, and teaching was to be stripped
away, and the Bible was to furnish direction for the conduct of
daily life. If some of the groups and persons mentioned above moved
from a literal Scriptural basis to a doctrine of spiritual inner authority, they were therefore not less but more critical of the elaboration
of public worship.

The Puritan would say with Paul, " This one thing I do." Taking the Scripture very simply as the Word of God, he disciplined himself to obey it. If altars and surplices and crucifixes were unknown in the New Testament Church, they are superfluous and indefensible in the Church of England. To require them, said John Gilby in 1581, was " to make Antichristes ragges a *sine qua non*." There were sinful superfluities in life and conduct too that must be cast out. The Puritans proposed a great simplification of worship and life. The brief span of our earthly years determines our eternal bliss or anguish. To loiter on our heavenly pilgrimage would be consummate folly. We husband our time, allowing no hour to slip by unprofitably. We use the things of this world only as aids toward the other. We eat and drink that we may be nourished for our rightful service. We engage in recreations only in so far as they contribute to our efficiency in God's work. Clothing is to be modest and free from showy and costly ornaments. The Puritan's life is a streamlined existence from which all superfluity is banished, and the frivolous and undisciplined activities of other men are excluded. He knows that at all times he has what Calvin called *negotium cum Deo* — business with God. God, the giver of life and of time, is to be obeyed and worshiped according to his Word. The Puritan has no use for days of celebration other than Sunday, which interrupt his proper work and service. " In the morning," wrote Samuel Sewell, April 1, 1719,

" I dehorted Sam Hirst, and Grindal Rawson, from playing Idle Tricks because 'twas first of April; they were the greatest fools that did so. N.E. men came hither to avoid anniversary days, the keeping of them such as the 25th of December. How displeasing it must be to God, the Giver of our Time, to keep anniversary days to play the fool."

If there is one universal principle in Puritanism, I suggest that we call it the principle of " economy." The Puritan loathed waste, both in worship and in daily employments. He was able to claim too that the New Testament was on his side. It knows nothing of the vestments and ornaments authorized in the ornaments rubric of the Prayer Book. It taught men to work, for the night comes when no man can work, and to redeem the time because the days are evil; and if a woman was approved for impulsively pouring out the precious ointment (in John, ch. 12), the lessons drawn from this by Puritan commentators did not disturb the pattern of teaching. It was for them simply a foreshadowing of Christ's priceless and redemptive sacrifice and a commendable act of devout love, with no general bearing upon economic behavior.

II

It is misleading to say that Puritanism is simply derived from the study of the Scriptures, or of the writings of Calvin or other Reformers. It has a background in older Christianity, and resembles some movements in other faiths. Many Puritans owed a good deal to the Stoics, who repeatedly urged the preciousness of time, with its opportunity for moral self-improvement. The Puritan habit of self-examination at evening, a daily checkup on failures and achievements, was a practice of Pythagoras and of the pupils of Confucius, and a commonplace of Stoic teaching. The Puritans had some of the qualities of the Pharisees in ancient Judaism. The multiple sects of Islam and of Hinduism afford examples of similar simplifications of religion in protest against the accretions of the past. Numerous earlier Christian groups and teachers show approximations to the English Puritan type. There are passages in Clement of Alexandria and in Tertullian that illustrate this. The Iconoclastic Movement in eighth century Byzantium has often been compared to the Puritan protest against images and other "idolatrous" objects in worship. Some of the medieval religious orders and sects have reminded historians, especially George Gordon Coulton, of the later Puritans. Saint Bernard of Clairvaux in his protest against William of Thierry over the superfluous space and showy ornaments in his church, exclaimed: "For God's sake, if men are not ashamed of these follies, why do they not shrink from the expense?" The Cistercians reduced the worship routine to something far less elaborate than that of the Cluniacs, practiced hard physical labor, and accused the Cluniacs of using "material ornaments" in worship, of eating too well and sleeping too long. The great John Gerson of Paris opposed the use of images and pictures as "perverting simple folk to idolatry." I point to parallels; but Dr. Coulton would discover the very ancestry of Puritanism in medieval piety. He has this to say:

"Puritanism is indeed not of one time but of most times and especially of most religious revivals. Its faults are simply the faults of exaggeration, an exaggerated belief in the value of religious phrases and religious deportment with an exaggerated depreciation of 'the world' in that narrow sense which was of hoary antiquity before the sixteenth century was born. . . . The Puritanism of the Reformation was the strictest and most logical attempt yet made to realize certain thoroughly medieval ideals" ("The High Ancestry of Puritanism," *Contemporary Review*, 1905. Republished in *Medieval Studies*, First Series, IV).

In the nature of the case there is, however, considerable difference between the "Puritanism" of celibates in religious orders and that of men in families engaged in callings of the world. Nor has it ever been made clear that Tudor Puritanism was specifically indebted to monasticism and the friars.

Others have found the ancestry of Puritanism in Anglo-Saxon as distinct from Norman England, and have considered its emergence as the revival of the Anglo-Saxon element in English life. This view may indeed claim support from utterances of some of the lesser sectarians of the Cromwellian period, especially the Levellers. A hundred years ago, it was tentatively put forward by John Stoughton, in the first volume of his *Religion in England* (Revised Edition, London, 1881), page 52:

"It is possible even that peculiarities of race and blood might have somewhat to do with the strong sympathies of the middle and lower classes, in a simple and unostentatious kind of religious worship. The plain and sturdy nature of the Anglo-Saxon was still pure, in a multitude of cases, from Norman admixture, in those ranks of society in which Puritanism most prevailed; and the Anglo-Saxon had ever been unfriendly to the ecclesiastical pomp of architecture and glittering ritual which delighted the Norman. Traditional opinions and sentiments opposed to the spirit of Romanism had been handed down through the Middle Ages from one generation to another of the English commonalty, in their homesteads and cottages, and probably as those opinions and sentiments had contributed to the outburst of Lollardism and helped on the cause of the Reformation, so also they ministered to the later development of principles proceeding further in the same direction. . . . Puritanism came only as the second stage of a progress of which the Reformation was the first."

The influence of Wyclif on the movement has been variously estimated. In many respects he anticipated the Puritan teachings, especially in his emphasis on the Bible as the guide of life and in his repudiation of the papacy. But Wyclif's followers were severely persecuted, and in the opening of the sixteenth century they consisted almost solely of humble tradesmen. John Strype and many later writers have presented evidence that the surviving Lollard groups were no negligible factor in promoting the spread of Tyndale's New Testament, and thus made some contribution to the rise of Protestantism in Henry VIII's reign. It is not clear, however, that they helped in any way to found English Puritanism, or that it felt strongly the inspiration of Wyclif. To say with Dr. Hensley Henson that "the Reformation, so far as it was a popular movement, was a Lollard movement" is, I think, wholly misleading; although we may agree with him that the Lollards, like the Puritans, held the necessity of Scriptural authority for all ecclesiastical arrangements. Richard Hooker was to combat this view against the Puritans of his day as Reginald Pecock, in his celebrated *Treatise Against Overmuch Blaming of the Clergy* (1455), had tried to do against the fifteenth century Lollards. Cranmer may have had the Lollard view of Scripture primarily in mind when he met the plea of John Hooper that kneeling be not required in the sacrament, with the statement:

"That what is not commanded in the Scripture is not lawful, is the root of the errors of the sects. . . . Kneeling is not enjoined in Scripture, neither is standing or sitting. Let them lie on the ground and eat their meat like Turks or Tartars."

Thomas Cuming Hall has argued for a clear distinction between Puritanism, which derived from Continental sources, and Dissent, which emerged early in medieval England, and was then chiefly expressed in Wyclifism. Dissent takes the Bible alone as authoritative. Every believing soul is aided by the indwelling Spirit in reading the Bible. The sacraments are for Dissent only pious symbols. On the other hand, in Puritanism, under Continental influence, churchly ideas are adhered to; the letter of Scripture is less important; sacraments and creeds are emphasized. The antiaesthetic element in Anglo-American religion comes from Dissent and not from Puritanism. Partly from poverty, more from the hatred of the expensive amusements of an oppressive landowning class, Dissent denounced the theater as sinful. In Dr. Hall's judgment, this nonecclesiastical or antiecclesiastical religion has never embraced less than one third of the English people.

To my mind, interpretations that derive Puritanism from the Anglo-Saxon element in England, as well as that which tries to separate it wholly from something called Dissent, are alike tendentious and unreliable. The argument from race would require evidence, far beyond that which is offered to us, of the continued separation of Saxon and Norman in England. The historian G. V. Lechler, in his valuable but now antiquated study *John Wycliff and His English Precursors,* took the view that Wyclif himself came from a district and a family that had remained pure Germans from the time of the Anglo-Saxon invasions. Actually he knew far too little about Wyclif's ancestors to justify this opinion. The most that we can say on the Saxon-anti-Norman origin of Puritanism is that Puritanism was associated with the rise of the middle class and the decline of the nobility, and that certain leftist elements in it applied the word "Norman" to the nobility as a term of abuse.

III

With respect to the connection of Puritanism with Continental Protestantism we are, however, on surer ground. The influence here was not wholly from the Reformed side, but also in part from the Lutheran side, of the Reformation. Readers of Luther will find the word "idolatry" frequently used with regard to many features of the late medieval church services. In 1522, Luther remarked, at the beginning of the fourth of his eight Wittenberg sermons:

"Images ought to be abolished if they are going to be worshiped. I wish they were abolished everywhere because they are abused."

He thought it would be better to give a poor man a gold piece than to give God a golden image. Yet in practice Luther retained very much that was medieval in worship, believing that what the Scripture did not condemn might still be kept in use. The Reformed leaders, on the other hand, tended to make the Scripture a negative rule, and to exclude from worship whatever was not enjoined or exemplified in Holy Writ. Many Puritans applied the Reformed principle with greater strictness than appears in the worship of the Continental churches.

Martin Bucer of Strasbourg, since he signed, and helped to negotiate, the Wittenberg Concord, 1536, may be classed as a Lutheran. Yet his temper was Puritanic, and his influence in England where he spent his last two years as an exile (1549–1551) was a formative factor in early Puritanism. In his *Censura,* or comments made on Cranmer's First Prayer Book, he held that the vestments authorized in it, though not sinful, are not desirable. He opposes kneeling at the sign of the cross and the use of prayers for the dead, and he wishes to see the altar replaced by a table. In other writings, notably his *De regno Christi,* he advocates a disciplined way of life quite congenial to Puritans. The emphasis he gives to the local congregation in his view of the Church brings him somewhat into line with the later Independents. August Lang has strongly argued the case for Bucer's Puritan influence upon John Bradford and others of his pupils, and regards him as a forerunner, if not a direct inspirer, of William Perkins, the Cambridge Puritan theologian.

Still nearer in some respects to the Puritans was John à Lasco (Jan Laski), the Polish reformer who was in England most of the time from 1548 to 1553. Placed in charge of a church of refugees in London, à Lasco elected not to use the Anglican liturgy in his services, and supported John Hooper in his opposition to the vestments. His introduction of "the prophecies" (group conferences of ministers and laymen for study and discussion) should be remembered in connection with the Puritan " prophesyings " of the early period of Elizabeth. It became necessary for Matthew Parker, Archbishop of Canterbury, to send word to Bishop John Parkhurst of Norwich " that the Queen's Majesty wills me to suppress those vain prophesyings." Parker's successor, Edmund Grindal, was deprived of his jurisdiction for his refusal to act likewise (1577). À Lasco, who was in substantial agreement with Zwingli, introduced in his church simple and untraditional procedures, enjoying Cranmer's full consent for this since no Englishmen were involved. He set up a Reformed Church discipline under elders, publicly installed all officers of the church, and in fact furnished a Puritan model of an Independent congregation.

The Reformation in Zurich under Zwingli's leadership was marked by the stripping of the worship forms to a bare minimum. In a kind of Puritan crusade, Zwingli had crucifixes, relics, pictures, altars, and candles removed from the churches. The venerated bones of saints were decently buried. The use of gold and silver ornaments and jewelry, and of expensive clothing, was prohibited, as were also gambling and carousing. The influence of Zwingli's great successor, Heinrich Bullinger, on the rise of English Puritanism would be hard to overstate. His hospitality to the exiles of Mary's reign who came to Zurich, his correspondence with these afterward, and the translation and authorized use in the Church of England of Bullinger's *Decades* (fifty sermons in translation, arranged in groups of ten), make it no exaggeration to say that he was the greatest Continental ally of Tudor Puritanism.

It was Calvin, however, whom the Puritans held in highest esteem as a theologian. Not only his *Institutes* but also many of his sermons and other writings were translated into English soon after their appearance. It is true that Anglican opponents of Puritanism sometimes quoted Calvin to refute Puritan opinions. Nevertheless in his thought and practice Calvin gave great encouragement to the main principles of Puritanism. The Arminian revision of Calvinism was resisted by many Puritans, and adopted by a few of them only when it was already widely espoused in Anglicanism. The outlines of the theocratic organization of Geneva under Calvin's direction were well known in England. " The Laws of Geneva " were translated into English by Robert Fells (1560). Calvin's Puritanism was less extreme than that of Zwingli, who, although himself a talented musician, ruthlessly suppressed even singing in the Church for the reason that in previous decades it had become extremely unedifying. Calvin promoted singing and appropriated this art to church use. He employed a liturgy that represented an extreme simplification of the Roman Mass. But he was emphatically negative on many medieval practices that remained in Lutheranism and in the Church of England. In 1550, he wrote to Melanchthon to protest against that Reformer's admission of some features of Charles V's *Interim,* by which candles, pictures, and other elements of medieval ritual were approved.

Here we have the same question that troubled the conscience of Thomas Sampson. It was the question of the adiaphora, the things nonessential or indifferent. " You extend the distinction of nonessentials too far," says Calvin in this letter, and he cites Paul's attitude to the Judaizers — " to whom we gave place . . . no, not for an hour " (Gal. 2:5). Calvin's correspondence with Bucer, Cranmer, and the Duke of Somerset indicates, I think we may say, that he was prepared to give place " for an hour " to the ritual elements in the Prayer Book which the Puritans criticized, but that he had no thought of authorizing permanent acquiescence in these. When he was consulted by the Marian exiles in Frankfort with regard to the Second Prayer Book, of which he had received a hastily made Latin translation, he wrote back to William Whittingham, January 31, 1555: " In the Anglican liturgy, as you described it to me, I see many tolerable stupidities (*tolerabiles ineptias*) "; he recommends that they " be endured for a time." He does not understand those who hanker after the " dregs of papistry," but he urges Whittingham's group to avoid wrangling. To take a peaceable and moderate course, while persistently seeking reform, was generally Calvin's prescription for his friends in trouble of conscience over forms of worship. When in January, 1561, he learned of iconoclastic riots in which churches had been invaded and relics destroyed by his

Huguenot followers in France, he wrote to restrain them: "God has never enjoined anyone to destroy idols, unless in his own house, or unless he is in authority in public."

It is easy to discover elements of Puritanism in the reign of Edward VI, and even in that of Henry VIII, but it was in the reign of Mary that it began to be clearly differentiated from other elements in the English religious scene, chiefly in the experiences of those who left the kingdom in fear of persecution. It was not, as has been argued without any weight of evidence by Christina Garrett, because they plotted revolution that the Marian exiles went abroad; nor was that the reason why so many Protestants who remained in England were burned to death. With a certain prudence, the exiles fled for their lives. At Frankfort the English congregation was divided into critics and partisans of the Second Prayer Book of Edward. The critics were Puritans and Knox was one of their chief leaders. He and his group had to take flight elsewhere, and he went to lead the refugee colony in Geneva. Many were in Zurich, feeding physically as well as spiritually at the tables of Bullinger and his associates. Hearing of the persecution at home, studying and writing and stimulating each other, the Puritan exiles became more Puritan. When Mary died, their return was dreaded by those who had acquiesced in her policies. Bishop John White at her funeral was apprehensive: "I warn you that the wolves be coming out of Geneva and other places in Germany, and have sent their books before them."

It was not long until they were active and prominent in the Church. Some who had more than a dash of Puritanism in their spirits became bishops. But the truly convinced and immovable ones boggled at the "Romish rags," or the episcopal jurisdiction, or something else that they held to be non-Scriptural in the Prayer Book or the polity of the Church. They had fled in fear of Mary, and Mary's persecutions fixed in the Puritan mind a peculiar loathing of Roman Catholicism. This extended to everything in worship, and the ornaments of worship that reminded them of "the grim wolf" and "the Babylonian woe." Many Anglicans were not less hostile to the papacy, without sharing the alerted fear of Rome characteristic of the Puritans. Whitgift's chaplain, William Barlow, described a Puritan as " a Protestant frayed out of his wittes."

A rough identification with Calvinism was made by the early hostile observers of Puritanism. This is interestingly stated by De Silva, the ambassador of Philip II of Spain, in 1568:

" Those who call themselves of the *religio purissima* go on increasing. They are the same as Calvinists and they are styled Puritans because they allow no ceremonies nor any forms save those which are authorized by the bare letter of the Gospels."

Thomas Fuller and John Heylin have dated the beginning of the use of the nickname " Puritan " about the year 1564, while Marshall M. Knappen gives the winter of 1567–1568 as the time of its origin. It gradually replaced the word " precisian," the term employed in the letters of Archbishop Parker. Englishmen soon had less reason to regard the Puritans as " the same as Calvinists." The Puritan Robert Brown had a different conception of the Church from that of Calvin, and, on the other hand, Archbishop John Whitgift out-Calvined Calvin in his statement of the doctrine of the Decrees of God (1595), yet engaged in a controversy with the Puritan Thomas Cartwright. Whitgift's theological opponents may have sometimes called him a Puritan, but this was the language of abuse, and the abuse of language. On the other hand, John Hooper, whose stand against Cranmer in Edward's reign and whose conception of Church reform mark him as a Puritan, was vastly more indebted to Bullinger than he was to Calvin. When Hooper was in prison, Calvin wrote to Bullinger, March 25, 1551, " I had rather he had not carried his opposition so far with regard to the cap and linen vestment, even though I do not approve of these." So while Calvin's conception of the adiaphora was stricter than that of Melanchthon, some of the Puritans were too strict for him.

IV

The Puritan's problems were moral rather than theological. His theology was not subtle or involved. The law of God, the grace of God, and man's response to these were primary, and they were dis-

coverable in Holy Scripture. English Puritanism produced no great
or original theologians. It rather assumed that the tasks of theology
had been done, and turned to the application of the doctrines of the
Reformation. The Puritan was not inclined to elaborate doctrinal
points, though he was exacting in his demands for piety. Dr. Knappen quotes from the works of Richard Greenham, a Cambridge
Elizabethan Puritan, this simple formulation:

> "They that willingly hear and joyfully embrace the doctrine that we
> are by law condemned for sin, by the gospel saved through faith in
> Christ, and thenceforth endeavor to have this world crucified unto us,
> and us to be crucified unto the world, and to become new creatures, shall
> also be saved and find mercy and peace."

Puritan preachers might extend the number of headings in their
sermons, but the topics they were genuinely concerned with in their
theology were few. God is to them an ever-present reality. They
may doubt their own salvation, but they do not doubt the fact of
God, and his manifestation not only in Scripture but in conscience
and experience. God is not to be trifled with. Our sins condemn
us, and we are hopeless without repentance and forgiveness.

Noteworthy is Greenham's phrase "to become new creatures."
Puritans wrote a great deal on the subject of conversion. In this
they anticipated the Pietists and the Evangelicals. Conversion for
them is a fundamental transformation of life in attitude and purpose. Baxter, in his *Call to the Unconverted* (1657), is careful to
distinguish it from merely "taking up some new opinion and falling
into some dividing party," or making vain resolutions of amendment.

> "It is not a small matter to bring an earthly mind to heaven, to show
> man the amiable excellence of God till he be taken up in such love to
> him that can never be quenched; to break the heart for sin, to make
> him fly for refuge to Christ."

The call to repentance, Baxter writes, is conveyed "in every leaf
of the blessed book of God," in every sermon, every motion of the
spirit, in the voice of conscience, in the examples of the godly, and
in the works of God in nature. It is all reasonable, for God is the God
of truth and reason.

"A man is never well in his wits till he be converted . . . nor knows the world, nor himself, nor what his business is on earth, so as to set himself about it, till he be converted."

Some Puritans referred feelingly to the anguish of the soul under the realization of divine wrath before deliverance comes. Perkins describes the symptoms:

"A change and alteration of the body as it were a burning agew — and it causes the entrails to rise, the liver to rowle in the body and it sets a great heat in the bones and consumes the flesh more than any sickness can do."

Young John Bunyan, while engaged in a game of tipcat on a Sunday, was arrested by a voice from heaven that said: "Wilt thou leave thy sins and go to heaven or have thy sins and go to hell?" This put him in "an exceeding maze."

"I looked up to heaven and was as if I had, with the eyes of my understanding, seen the Lord Jesus looking down upon me, and being very hotly displeased with me, and as if he did severely threaten me with some grievous punishment for these and my other ungodly practices."

But when it was clear that his sins were forgiven, Bunyan was like his own Pilgrim, whose burden of sin rolled away at the foot of the cross: "Then Christian gave three leaps for joy, and went on singing." The Puritan may have had his moods of depression, but ordinarily he took these as a part of his education in godliness and looked for a break in the clouds. God in his wrath would remember mercy.

The doctrine of the two covenants — of works and of grace — was characteristic of Puritan theology. Elements of the Covenant (or Federal) Theology appear in numerous sixteenth century Continental Reformed writers, such as Heinrich Bullinger and Caspar Olevianus. The Scottish national covenants were apparently associated with the development of this doctrine, and the first principal of Edinburgh University, Robert Rollock, wrote an early treatise on the subject, *De foedere Dei et de sacramentis* (1596). William Perkins in *The Golden Chain* (Latin, 1590; English, 1591), John Preston in *The New Covenant* (1629), and William Ames in *The Marrow of Sacred Divinity* (Latin, 1629; English, 1642) were among the Puritan predecessors of John Cocceius, whose *De foedere* (1648) is usually regarded as the most important treatise in this field. Later Puritans, such as John Owen and Richard Baxter in various works, and William Strong in *Discourse of the Two Covenants* (1678), maintained the ascendancy of the doctrine through the seventeenth century. These writers, with Jonathan Edwards after them, exhibit considerable variation in detail in their expositions of the covenants. Regardless of this diversity, the doctrine served the purpose of checking the tendency in Calvinism to ascribe to God an arbitrary and unpredictable role in salvation. In the Covenant Theology, God has assumed obligations to the believer.

" Man's chief end is to glorify God, and to enjoy him forever." God is not only to be worshiped and obeyed but to be enjoyed, now and hereafter. The awareness of God's presence is what gives meaning and zest to life. Amid the distresses of the Restoration, Baxter wrote:

" If I had not a God to know and think on, to love and honour, to seek and serve, what had I to do with my understanding, will, and all my powers? What should I do with life and time? . . . What could I find to do in the world that is worthy of a man? " (*The Mischief of Self-ignorance,* p. 111. London, 1662).

John Howe, another of the ejected Puritans of 1662, wrote a *Treatise of Delighting in God*; and Matthew Henry, the commentator read by our grandfathers, found the law of the Lord his delight. In *The Pleasantness of the Religious Life* he re-echoes the Puritan warnings against seeking joy in artificial and time-wasting amusements, and affirms that the pleasures of religion are solid and substantial and not painted on; they are gold and not gilded over; they are enduring. By true religion a man has the delight of being master of his own thoughts, he lives in kindly relationships with others, and in communion with God, who " speaks freely to us as a man to his friend." Prayer and psalm-singing are sources of gladness and " the Lord's day a pleasant day of holy rest and holy joy." I do not find in the Puritans that " lack of Christian joy in the sense of the Letter to the Philippians " which is alleged of them by Joseph Chambon (*Der Puritanismus,* p. 279). Perhaps gladness was not their habitual mood. But the notion that they were purveyors of a sad religion is what may be called in seventeenth century language a " vulgar error." Men who believe that the everlasting God is their refuge and that no crisis can place them beyond the range of his help are not habitually sad. Thomas Becon, in *The Jewel of Joy,* exclaimed: " O the unoutspeakable goodness of God toward men "; and Thomas Adams in a sermon has the immortal sentence, most true to Puritan experience, " Man's extremity is God's opportunity."

A pessimist, we are told, is a man who has been in conversation with an optimist. We have all heard pulpit discourses on joy in the religious life that were not entirely convincing. Perhaps many Puritan preachers, in common with others, adopted that rhythmical utterance that we call the holy whine, and failed to make real to their hearers that joy in God which is frequently expressed in their writings.

The Puritan's religion was of the kind described by John Wesley as " Scriptural holiness." Holiness is a favorite word in the Puritan vocabulary, but more often the term used for piety is " godliness." John Owen has a treatise on *The Sanctification of Believers* in which the Puritan notion of a holy or godly life can be readily discovered. Owen does not, as some Puritans did, present a routine of daily devotions. He defines holiness as " a spiritual habit," not a series of outward acts. It is a principle of spiritual life and grace infused into our souls, constantly abiding there, and the cause of all acts of holiness. He appears to feel that the devout may attain to a perpetual state of holiness: " This abideth in us and in all that are sanctified, whence they are always holy." He does not assert, however, that this abiding state of holiness is one of sinlessness.

V

The Puritan combined this exalted quest with the various activities of secular life. The vocation by which he earned his daily bread was never thought of as outside the province of religion, or to be detached or exempted from the requirements of religion. When Matthew Henry was twenty-four years old, he set down, as did many other Puritans in youth, a series of vows which he solemnly undertook to fulfill. The most comprehensive of these self-imposed obligations reads: " I do likewise devote and dedicate unto the Lord my whole self, all I am, all I have, and all I can do." The things that Matthew Henry could do included the writing of the most celebrated of Puritan commentaries on the Scriptures. Philip Doddridge said that Henry was the only commentator who deserved to be read entirely through. It is characteristic that when Matthew Henry writes about the obligation of Adam to dress and keep the Garden of Eden, he takes occasion to remark:

" Secular employments will very well consist with a state of innocency and a life of communion with God. The sons and heirs of heaven while they are here in the world have something to do about this earth which must have its share of their time and thoughts; and if they do it with an eye to God, they are as truly serving him in it as when they are upon their knees."

This doctrine was no discovery of the Puritans. There are similar expressions in some of the medieval mystics, in Luther and the other Reformers, and in the discourses of Saint Theresa of Avila. But the Puritans sensed with peculiar keenness the close relationship between religious experience and common, everyday duties. This fact is the more significant for history because they lived in an era of economic expansion and change, and of political revolution. They knew that they had " something to do about this earth," and they brought the power of religious conviction into the momentous struggles of the age.

We have seen a modern tendency to look upon the Puritans as historically important mainly for their political and economic attitudes. If Cartwright, or Perkins, or Bunyan, or Baxter could see what secular historians have written about them, they would be greatly surprised. Now, much of this type of historical work has its own validity. Puritanism has had important bearings upon the evo-

lution of modern secular life. It is one thing to recognize this outcome of what the Puritans thought; it is quite another thing to assume that they used religion as a means to political or economic
ends. Their primary motives and interests lay in the religious realm.
" In doing good," says Baxter, " prefer the souls of men before the
body " unless the man is drowning or famishing (*The Christian Directory,* Part I, ch. iii). " Be not so diligent in thy particular calling
that thou neglect the duties of thy general calling as a Christian,"
says Thomas Gouge (*The Christian Direction,* " How to Walk with
God All the Day Long," ch. xii).

Deeply convinced of the sovereignty of God over all human affairs, Puritans were inclined to call in question the sovereignty of
kings. The Geneva Bible, with which they were familiar, is furnished with marginal notes, many of which call to special attention
the Scriptural instances of wicked, indulgent, and misguided kings.
Or, if they read, for example, the prophecy of Daniel, and turned to
Calvin's commentary on this book for an interpretation of the character of Darius, they would find this sweeping judgment:

" If anyone could enter into the hearts of kings, he would find scarcely
one in a hundred who does not despise everything divine. Although they
confess themselves to enjoy their throne by the grace of God, as we have
previously remarked, yet they wish to be adored in his stead. We now
see how easily flatterers persuade kings to do whatever seems likely to
extol their magnificence."

Calvin wished to see kings restrained by the activity of magistrates
who were defenders of the liberties of the people. Similarly, the
Puritans, in general, turned for relief from royal policies to the activities of Parliament. Tudor Parliaments had been rather easily persuaded to act in accordance with the royal will; yet the institution
of Parliament remained intact and had possibilities for another
course of action. During the reign of Elizabeth I we have numerous
efforts to bring about a reform of the Church in accordance with
Puritan ideals by action of Parliament. No less than six bills were introduced into Parliament in 1566, setting forth proposals for altera-
tions in worship and reform of abuses connected with Church ben-

efices. Of the parliamentary spokesmen of Puritanism the most
aggressive were Walter Strickland and Peter Wentworth. Frequently
they clashed with the royal policy. In a speech in the opening session of the Parliament of 1576, Wentworth boldly affirmed the rights
of the House against the royal pressure:

"I find written in a little volume . . . 'Sweet is the name of liberty,
but the thing itself . . . beyond all inestimable treasure.'"

Free speech, he charges, has been infringed:

"Without this it is a scorn and mockery to call it a parliament house,
for in truth it is none, but is a very school of flattery and dissimulation."

When reforms in religion are proposed in Parliament, a whisper is
circulated, "The queen liketh not of it," or messages of disapproval
come to the House, "greatly to Her Majesty's dishonour." He regards the messages as emanating from the bishops. Quoting thirteenth century Bracton's *De legibus Angliae,* he states that the
king ought to be under the law.

"It is a great part of our duty to maintain the freedom of consultation
and speech. . . . It is better that one should be hanged than that this
noble state should be subverted."

Wentworth was asserting parliamentary authority in religion over
that of the bishops, and complete freedom of utterance for criticisms
of the Elizabethan settlement on the floor of Parliament. For this he
was sent to the Tower for a month. It was but an incident in the
long-continued effort on the part of the Presbyterian party and their
political supporters to alter the whole structure of the Church, by
political enactment. If we read closely the story of the parliaments of
Elizabeth, we find less surprising the alliance of Puritanism with
parliamentary resistance to the king under the Stuarts.

Elizabeth managed her Parliament with a certain adroitness and
was not too insistent on explicit acknowledgment of royal authority.
King James I, however, had imbibed the notion of divine-right absolute monarchy, and proceeded to instruct his subjects in this high

doctrine. He told the Parliament of 1610 that "in the Scriptures kings are called gods so that their power after a certain relation is compared to divine power," and drew the conclusion that:

"As to dispute what God may do in blasphemy . . . so is it sedition in subjects to dispute what a king may do in the height of his power. . . . I would wish you to be careful that you do not meddle with the main points of government. That is my craft."

James's frank and astonishing mystical reverence for himself as a king was shared by numerous Anglican divines. But an alliance was established between the Puritans and the Parliament in opposition to the royal claim, and by 1621 we have a crisis in which James complains that the Commoners are beginning to debate publicly of things too high for them, to the dishonor of the royal prerogative. The Commons asserted its own "liberties, privileges, and jurisdictions" as "the ancient and undoubted first right and inheritance of the subjects of England." This protestation of December, 1621, was followed by the Petition of Right, presented to King Charles I in April, 1628. The arbitrary government of Charles and the severe punishment inflicted upon his opponents in Church and State rendered firm the opposition to monarchical absolutism, and in the 1640's monarchy and episcopacy tumbled down together.

VI

How far would Puritanism go in its rejection of divine-right absolutism? The test came in 1648–1649. The Presbyterians in Parliament wished to bring the king to terms, and effect a limited monarchy. It was only when Cromwell sent Colonel Pride to exclude from Parliament the members of the Presbyterian party that those measures could be authorized in it which resulted in the execution of the king (January 29, 1649). Although Cromwell's conduct in all this was both ungenerous and imprudent, perhaps it was his exaggerated sense of mission that carried him beyond the course of reason. He did not realize that in Pride's Purge he was dividing the forces of political Puritanism, or that he was entering on a fatal series of experiments in arbitrary government that must lead to the ruin of the Puritan cause.

Broadly speaking, it was the Presbyterian conception of government rather than that of Cromwell that triumphed forty years later in the Bill of Rights, by which Parliament, " vindicating and asserting their ancient rights and liberties," abolished " the pretended power of suspending laws by regal authority," and finally set the pattern of limited monarchy for England. Meanwhile, Anglicanism had been restored and Puritanism rejected. There would have been no Great Revolution of 1688–1689 on the surviving strength of Puritan political doctrine alone. The Stuarts could always be counted upon to blunder fatally, and it was because James II attempted to bring England once more into the orbit of the papacy that he was rejected by the bishops and the people. Nevertheless, the fact that the Puritans were consistently opposed to the high pretensions of kings helped materially to confirm England in its natural course toward the establishment of limited monarchy.

Some whom we class as Puritans not only assailed monarchy but sought to abolish the old class structure. Certain groups like the Levelers felt a particular grievance against the nobility and the privileged classes. It was these folk who liked to denounce the " Normans," and the nobility as their successors. Some groups and individuals made a point of vilifying the universities and all their alumni. On July 18, 1573, Archbishop Parker wrote to Lord Burleigh,

" Surely if this fond faction be applauded to or borne with, it will fall out to a popularity and, as wise men think, it will be the overthrow of all the nobility."

John Strype, quoting this in his *Life of Matthew Parker,* explains that by " popularity " Parker meant " a parity and equality in the State as well as in the Church." Parker was seeking to arouse Burleigh against the Puritans by pointing to the possibility of danger to Burleigh's class as well as to his own. But with regard to the traditional stratification of society, many of the Puritans were conservative enough. One may support a system of stratification on a functional argument, without implying a moral subordination and without denying rights to the "lower" orders of society. Though William Perkins was a warm supporter of the monarchy as it was under Elizabeth, he was intensely concerned for the well-being of all classes of subjects and their happy functioning in their callings, each in his station and degree. Cromwell himself deplored the agitation of the Levellers and desired that the traditional social classes be maintained. The Levellers, in turn, in their tracts referred to Cromwell's as "the old tyrannical Norman government." (See W. Schenk, *The Concern for Social Justice in the Puritan Revolution,* pp. 28 ff., 67 f. London and New York, 1948.)

Thus the Puritans (taking the word in its broad sense) offer a variety of political and social judgments, even though they carefully support them all by reference to the Bible. It is always a mistake to assume that the Puritan is a man of one book. He may have continually protested that he was deriving his ideas from the Bible, while he was also, consciously or unconsciously, reflecting much that he had read in classical or modern writers; sometimes he exhibits too a familiar knowledge of medieval scholastic treatments of political and economic themes.

VII

The Puritan conception of economic duty has been the subject of much discussion and inquiry since Max Weber's study of *Protestantism and the Spirit of Capitalism,* which first appeared in 1904–1905. Weber's suggestions of the intimate relation of Calvinism and capitalism in history were actually put forth far more cautiously than many people now suppose. Yet he confused the issue somewhat by the assumptions that Puritanism is identical with Calvinism and that Benjamin Franklin offers a suitable sample of Puritan ethics. Many have written to modify or controvert the thesis of Weber; and yet, so far as the Puritans are concerned, the whole subject of economic ethics requires fuller examination than has been given to it. The strength of Puritanism lay in the rising middle class, who were naturally hospitable to its teaching on thrift and industry. But those who habitually heard Puritan sermons would not fail to have their consciences aroused, or, at any rate, prodded, on the obligation to serve, rather than the opportunity for gain, in the business life. For the Puritan, no special virtue lay in poverty itself; but great dangers lay in riches, in both getting and spending, and in the possession of what they called " abundance " as distinct from a necessary sustenance. Perkins, in his *Cases of Conscience,* states that it is a sin to seek abundance; it is a hazard to salvation, and one of its fruits is " diffidence," or a lack of faith in the power of God. On the topic of the calling, Perkins offers a comment which I think would be subscribed to by practically all those whom we include under the general name of Puritan. It is as follows:

" The end of a man's calling is not to gather riches for himself or his family or the poor, but to serve God in serving of man, and in seeking the good of all men; and to this end men must apply their lives and labors."

Here in a nutshell is the Puritan creed for economic life. This conception excluded all waste of goods, of time, and of energy. " Six days shalt thou labor " was quite as important as the other part of that Commandment. Yet there was no hesitancy over, or casuistical modification of, the Sabbath rest required in that other part. Calvin had warned against a " Jewish rigor " in the regulation of Sunday, but most Puritans were rigorous on this point of the law. It has been shown that in earlier centuries pious Englishmen and Scots (Irish evidence might also be adduced) were often greatly concerned over the sanctity of the day of rest. Gainful work was excluded, and with it recreation. It was not only the Puritans, of course, who were displeased by James I's *Book of Sports* (1618), prescribing Sunday afternoon physical training, but they were especially offended.

It ought to be remembered that while they denounced and shunned Sunday recreation, they had no inclination to banish all recreation. In fact, they gave to it a noteworthy place in their teachings. They wrote about recreation with the gravity of a modern sociologist, from their own religious point of view, carefully distinguishing health-giving exercises and relaxations from time-wasting, energy-consuming, purposeless amusements; and with these excluding violent games and brutal sports. Macaulay's oft-repeated quip, " The Puritans hated bearbaiting not because it gave pain to the bear but because it gave pleasure to the spectators," completely evades the truth of the matter, which Puritan writers treat very differently. They loathed the inhumanity of bearbaiting and other sports involving cruelty, and were unhappy because men sank so low as to find pleasure in occasioning pain to God's creatures.

" What Christian heart [wrote Philip Stubbes] can take pleasure to see one poor beast to rend, tear, and kill another, and all for his foolish pleasure? And although they be bloody beasts to mankind and seek his destruction, yet we are not to abuse them, for His sake who made them and whose creatures they are."

Recreation, for the Puritan, like all other activities, is subordinated to life's main objectives. We should play when necessary in order to work more effectively in the service of God and man.

Nor is a man's success in gaining wealth the measure of God's favor: it may be the measure of his own villainy. Says Thomas Adams in his sermon on " God's Bounty " (Prov. 3:16):

" For us, beloved, we teach you not to cast away the bag, but covetousness. We bid you use the world, but enjoy the Lord. . . . It is easy for a man to be rich who will make his conscience poor. He that will defraud, forswear, bribe, oppress, serve the time, use, abuse, all men, all things, swallow any wickedness, cannot escape riches. . . . Wealth comes not easily, not quickly to the honest doer. . . . Of riches let us never desire more than an honest man may well bear away. I had rather be a miserable saint than a prosperous sinner."

It is true that wealth is also the God-given fruit of industry. Yet it cannot be said to be the end for which we work. The end is the good we may achieve by the work itself and by the beneficent use of the wealth it produces. The Puritan preacher was, in fact, fond of warning the rich of their responsibilities, and often ingenious in devising philanthropic projects by which they might helpfully part with their possessions.

Baxter, in his great work on casuistry, *The Christian Directory,* treats the economic duties in great detail. He refuses to say that all love of riches is sin, since riches may enable us to relieve our needy brethren and to promote good works for Church and State. But it is sinful to seek riches merely to feed the flesh and satisfy its desires, or to gratify our pride. Amid a great deal of specific direction of this sort, he condemns desiring more than is needful or useful, and being more careful to provide a worldly than a heavenly portion for children and friends (Part I, ch. iv). In an ample discussion of "the redeeming of time," Baxter remarks:

"Time must be redeemed from worldly business and commodity when matters of greater weight do require it, trades and profit must stand by when God calls us by necessity or otherwise to greater things. Martha should not so much as trouble herself in providing meat for Christ and his followers to eat when Christ is offering her food for her soul, and she should with Mary have been adoring at his feet" (Part I, ch. v, in *Practical Works,* I, 231).

We often find devotional writers (this is exemplified in a good many medieval mystics) venturing to take the side of Martha against Mary, and we might have expected as much at least from the Puritan, who is alleged to be an activist. Joseph Chambon has referred to "the undue prominence of the Martha type" in Puritanism (*Der Puritanismus,* p. 279). Yet Richard Baxter, who so often appealed for active goodness, specifically judges Martha guilty of forsaking her true duty. Perhaps Meister Eckhart and Saint Theresa held a brief for Martha mainly because their immediate hearers were by habit favorers of Mary, while Baxter well knew that Martha's role was the preference of a great many to whom he appealed. Yet it is fair to cite this passage in evidence of one broad and universal fact with regard to the Puritan leaders. When treating of secular things, they do not compromise with the spirit of secularity. Religious devotion comes first; it limits and governs secular actions.

Of course, the Puritan, who was blessed in his basket and his store, and who proved the truth of the saying that the hand of the diligent makes rich, faced the base temptation to become a loafer. Let me permit myself one more quotation from Baxter:

" Will not riches excuse one from laboring in a calling? No, but rather bind them to it the more, for he that hath most wages from God should do him most work " (*Practical Works,* I, 375).

The Puritan does not retire on his accumulated fortune into a life of shameful ease.

" The Intellectual Failure of Puritanism " is the title of a chapter in H. Hensley Henson's *Puritanism in England* (1912). Since this book was written, our respect for Puritan learning has been vastly augmented by the weighty researches of numerous specialists. But learning is not the measure of intellectual greatness; and it is doubtful if the Puritans possessed an intellectual power comparable to their learning. It is true that Bunyan and Milton were the greatest literary geniuses of their time, and in their own crafts have not been surpassed in other times, but these two excepted, the Puritans were not rich in genius. In general, the Puritan intelligence exercised itself in controversies or in sermons, or writings of a homiletical type, and these contain very few literary gems. Thomas Adams has been called the Puritan Shakespeare; but he wrote no plays, and if he had written any, they would have been in one respect more like those of Ben Jonson than like those of Shakespeare. He cared more than Shakespeare did for mere learning. His sermons are sprinkled with fragments of the classics and odd scraps of book knowledge, while, like other Puritans, he does not fail to search the heart and probe the conscience. For a truly eminent Puritan theologian we must turn to Jonathan Edwards in eighteenth century New England.

VIII

Many of their contemporaries saw in the Puritans a certain sanctimoniousness and unreality of piety, if not out-and-out hypocrisy and false pretense. The *Discourse Concerning Puritans* quoted earlier complains that the Bishop of Down and Connor had described them as

" wringing their necks awry, lifting up the white of their eyes at the sight of some vanity, giving great groans, crying out against this sin and that sin in their superiors."

Samuel Butler's witty doggerel poem "Hudibras" did much to popularize the view that Puritans were hypocrites, and perhaps still helps to maintain it. Butler, a Roman Catholic in sympathy, had seen the late Cromwellian Puritanism, when the success of the movement had probably attracted to it many pretenders who mouthed the Puritan phrases. There is a fringe of pretense around every sincere movement. But to regard all Puritans as religious pretenders would be a judgment too absurd for discussion.

A more common charge against them nowadays is that they had no regard for the beautiful and were hostile to art. Sidney Dark (in *The Passing of Puritanism*, London, 1940) puts this strongly: "But to the Puritan the beauty of holiness would have seemed a blasphemous suggestion. Beauty was the invention of the devil." This charge is an invention of the class of interpreters to which Mr. Dark belongs. Actually the beauty of holiness was something like a favorite theme of Puritan hortative writers. But, as Joseph Crouch earlier pointed out in his *Puritanism and Art,* their conception of the beauty of holiness differed from that of Archbishop Laud, for whom the phrase referred to the external ornaments of the church. Crouch quotes an unnamed and unpleasant writer who illustrates the point by a reference to the sufferings of William Prynne:

"Prynne with his ears twice sawed from his head was excusable in not quite appreciating the music of the spheres. . . . Such things rather impeded the popular appreciation of Laud's upholstery of holiness."

It is not unlikely that the psalmist who wrote, "O worship the Lord in the beauty of holiness," had indeed in mind the fair and clean garments becoming to those present in the solemn assembly. I am not here concerned with the beauty or holiness of the vestments favored by Laud, nor would I suggest any necessary relation between High-Church attitudes on these matters and the punishment of unacceptable authors by the removal of their ears. But I believe that typical Puritans cared for both beauty and holiness, and particularly insisted that the two should be kept together.

As one would expect, the Puritan's conception of beauty was one that stemmed from his religion, from his awareness of God, of the awful beauty of creation, and of the orderly functioning of God's works. The enjoyment of a beautiful thing in a secular frame of mind is sin; and sin is not beautiful! It is ugly and loathsome, and a violation of the divinely ordained sweet correspondence of things.

The Puritans had indeed their artistic interests and their canons of art. Many of their houses displayed tastefully selected pictures, statuary, and tapestries. Lucy Hutchinson describes her husband, Colonel John Hutchinson, one of the Regicides, who died in prison in 1664, as expert in knowledge of painting, sculpture, and all the liberal arts. Cromwell was extremely fond of music, and an admirer of Titian's pictures. Inigo Jones was employed by Archbishop Laud to deface the Gothic of old St. Paul's by a Grecian portico with Corinthian pillars; he was employed in the Commonwealth period to do matchless interiors for the Earl of Pembroke at Wilton. What the Puritans attacked was the art objects in churches which they supposed to be occasions of idolatry and superstition. In 1643, Parliament required the removal of altars, pictures of Persons of the Trinity, of the Virgin Mary and of saints, and superstitious inscriptions. Figures of dead persons not taken for saints were to remain. In all this the Puritans should have been more discriminating. Yet it is the fact of the matter that they were not either Philistines or crude iconoclasts. They believed that a picture of God was dishonoring to God, and they acted on this belief.

The costumes of the Puritans are an index to their conception of art. While inventories show that some of them had rich wardrobes, generally in contrast to the curled locks and colorful apparel of the Cavaliers, they dressed plainly. But the typical Puritan garb is certainly not ugly. It has the beauty of functional fitness and economy. Artistically the Puritan doublet and hose had great advantages over the prevailing modern suit of clothes, which, however, is similarly monotonous in color. The clothing Puritans wore had character, and expressed the character of the wearers. So their conceptions of art and the beautiful excluded superfluity and mere external decoration. The integration of life under the will of God extended to art, and beauty was something not secular but related to the divine law in the universe. John Preston speaks of beauty in terms of the integrity and symmetry of a thing. A favorite word of some Puritans was *eutaxia,* Englished as " eutaxie," orderliness. " Let not," says Thomas Adams, " God's eutaxie, order, by our frivolous scruples be brought to ataxy, confusion."

Undoubtedly the Puritans feared and warned against the temptations of external beauty. They were also severe critics of dancing and stage plays. The condemnation of the theater by Christian moralists was of course nothing new; and here the prevailing Puritan view was shared by a great many Anglicans, some as remote from Puritanism as Jeremy Collier and William Law. Also, in the great majority of Puritan attacks upon the stage, the reference is not to the art but to its abuses. It is not the theater but *this* theater that is usually condemned. When Stephen Gosson turned from the theater to the Church, he wrote a sprightly attack upon the abuses, not the art, of the stage (*The School of Abuse,* 1579). Philip Stubbes, in *The Anatomy of Abuses* (1583), assailed the theater for the sins that attended it, and fifty years later William Prynne is even more hostile (*Histriomastix,* 1633). Between these writers came Shakespeare, of whose plays contemporary religious authors made no use.

Yet it must be said that there was little appreciation of drama by Puritans. Milton is in this an exception. Apparently most Puritans were too much shocked by the evils of the stage to look for its merits. Baxter is typical in condemning even the reading of stage plays as a waste of time. Dr. Percy A. Scholes, who (in *Puritanism and Music in England and New England*) has examined the whole question of Puritanism and the arts with meticulous care, points out that Stubbes was in church connection a loyal Anglican though from his opinions he is usually classed as a Puritan. Stubbes had the same critical approach to music that he had to plays. He writes:

" I say of Musick as Plato, Aristotle and Galen and many others have said of it; that it is very ill for young heds, for a certain kinde of nice smoothe swetnes in alluring the auditry to nicenes, effeminacie, pusillanimitie, and loathsomeness of life."

But the reference here is to music accompanying " filthie dancing," not to that by which a man is diverted from his cares at home. Regarding the latter, Stubbes has only praise:

" I grant Musick is a good gift of God, and that it delighteth both man and beast, reviveth the spirits, comforteth the hart and maketh it readier to serve God. . . . Used for man's private recreation Musick is very laudable."

The dancing he condemns is "dancing as it is used (or rather abused) in these daies," attended as it is by "baudye gestures"; just as Perkins refers to "dancing in these dayes" as "the very bellowes of Lust."

Most of us would not be a whit less unfavorable to the kind of dancing, or in many cases the kind of plays, these men were condemning. But their fault was (and ours may be) that they generally took no pains to reform the abuses of these arts and recreations. They were often content to reject what others did, not to seek its replacement. This is less true of music, in which many of them took a positive interest. But in general the dance and the theater were not serious enough for the Puritan. They demanded more time than they deserved from the Christian hastening on his way to heaven; and they were not conducive to that "heavenly-mindedness" which Baxter, Gouge, and others extolled. Those who find life dreary without these recreations suppose that Puritans lived a dreary life. This does not necessarily follow. They avoided the fatigue of the pleasure seeker whose "toiling pleasure sickens into pain." We read of Colonel Hutchinson that "he never was at any time idle, and hated to see anyone else so," but also that "he was naturally cheerful" and "everything that it was necessary for him to do he did with delight." Though "he could dance admirably well," he desisted from it, but cultivated his "great love of music, and often diverted himself with a viol, on which he played masterly."

IX

The Puritan austerity is not, then, basically a negation of life or of art. It is rather a consequence of that principle of economy to which attention was called above. But of necessity the application of this principle involved negations. It involved the exclusion of whatever was deemed a hindrance to the heavenly voyager. The accent was laid too much on these rejections. Often in controversy the Puritan so pressed his negations that he failed to affirm the good life in its fullness; and often he impoverished public worship. It is not easy to give a balanced judgment here. The anti-Puritan animus still finds popular expression, and is shared by the sons of pleasure and the lovers of ceremonial. We have a right to criticize many Puritans for pruning the tree too closely. But it is only folly to suppose that there should be no pruning. Whether we look at worship or at conduct, something corresponding to the Puritan criticism is always needful. Worship deteriorates under a growth of uncensored ceremonial, just as morality dissolves where discipline is neglected. To give the Puritan his due, he was primarily concerned with great matters — the renewal of the soul in God, a conscience void of offense, the will of God for Church and society — even though things secondary and peripheral to these sometimes received his grave attention.

All in all, Puritanism has been profitable to the modern world, especially the Anglo-Saxon world, which alone felt its direct impact. The good things in it are coming to fresh recognition and appreciation by scholars today. It was not the whole of Christianity, since it was weak in the expression of charity. But it may be that in life and worship the time is ripe for a kindlier and wiser utterance of some of the old Puritan criticisms and affirmations.

GERMAN PIETISM

I

The history of that movement in Protestantism commonly called Pietism has received little attention from writers in our language. A speaker who would mention it in any general group would probably have to guard against the current prejudice under which the word " piety " suffers. This word for many carries the suggestion of stuffiness, pretension, and a kind of religious anemia. Now " piety " was a good, honest word among the ancient pagans and early Christians. The adjective *pius* which Vergil attaches as a badge of honor to his epic hero was adopted as a personal name; it was borne by a bishop of Rome about A.D. 140-155. The Greek word *eusebeia,* which is Latinized as *pietas,* appears more than a dozen times in the New Testament. The Authorized Version usually renders it " godliness." The Revised Standard Version also uses " piety " or " religion." The basic thought is that of dutifulness, especially toward a deity. It was of course possible, as we see in II Tim. 3:5, to have " the form of *eusebeia* " while denying " the power of it "; and the professors of piety have often exhibited the form where they have not convinced others of the power. The thought of power is associated with that of piety also in Acts 3:12, where, after the healing of the cripple who sat for alms at the Beautiful Gate, Peter says to the astonished onlookers, " Why do you stare at us, as though by our own power or piety [*eusebeia*] we had made him walk? " In the German Pietists, we see again piety associated with spiritual power; and, like Peter, they would ascribe to the power of God all the good results of their labors.

The Pietist movement took its rise shortly after the Thirty Years' War, which spread physical devastation and human degradation through most of Germany. This disastrous conflict at the time (1618–1648) called forth little response from the churches that could suggest a favorable religious forecast. The invigorating conceptions of the Reformation had been systematized, and debilitated, in Lutheran scholasticism. The very debates in theology were skirmishes in corners of the field, unlike the larger controversies of another generation. The sufferings of war seem not to have stimulated the churches to any great effort toward the relief and comfort of the sufferers. If John Valentine Andreae undertook such labors at Calw, he had almost no imitators. A few were interested in the cause of Christian unity, such as George Calixtus, the leader of the so-called Syncretists, and the indomitable Scot, John Dury, who for half a century bore witness to the gospel of unity, mainly on the Continent. But no marked interest attended these efforts. Religious life was low, and the ministry generally ill-equipped to stir it to new vigor.

The apostle of the Pietist revival was Philipp Jakob Spener (1635–1705). When the Peace of Westphalia brought the war to an end, Spener was a boy of thirteen. Rappoltsweiler, Upper Alsace, where he was born and spent his boyhood, escaped the general ruin, and he lived a sheltered and privileged life. He early received strong religious impressions from both his parents and, more especially, from his godmother, the Countess of Rappoltstein. Joachim Stoll, the pastor of Rappoltstein, and later Spener's brother-in-law, religiously guided the growing boy, and initiated him into the Greek language. The Baron von Canstein, who wrote the first *Life of Spener* (1740), once asked him whether he ever was a bad boy. He admitted that he had once, when he was twelve, been induced to join in a dance; but he had been immediately overtaken by pangs of conscience (*Angst*), and broke from the dancing throng — never to dance again. This incident illustrates the naïve innocence and austere discipline of his boyhood, also perhaps the shyness that would be natural in a child so socially protected as Spener was. A psychologically trained student wrote a class paper on Spener in which he was represented as a life-long victim of timidity. This view involves some dubious conjectures. He never was so timid as to abandon his principles when attacked. But he grew up a grave and studious youth, and when he went to the University of Strasbourg, he avoided the student games and pleasures. He took an interest in history and heraldry, and was stimulated by his teachers religiously as well as intellectually. His master's thesis (1653) was an attack on Hobbes, entitled *On the Conformation of the Rational Nature to the Creator.*

He visited France in 1656 and, after other activities, in 1659 he started on an academic pilgrimage that began with Basel and was continued in Geneva. An illness caused his stay in Geneva to be protracted, and the Lutheran theology he had willingly imbibed at Strasbourg was fertilized by Calvinism. Similar had been the experience of John Valentine Andreae, who almost rapturously described the Christian community of Geneva fifty years before Spener's visit, and was moved by his observation of it to write his celebrated *Christianopolis* (1619). Though he remained a zealous Lutheran, Spener too was warm in his admiration for Geneva. He formed a friendship with a professor of history there, a devout Waldensian, Antoine Leger, who shared his hobby of heraldry. In Geneva he also met the celebrated ex-Jesuit Jean de Labadie (d. 1674), who had just entered upon a seven-year residence there and was vehemently preaching repentance and regeneration. Labadie atempted to found a new church of the regenerate, on the primitive model, and Spener attended some of his meetings. It is likely that he was much impressed by Labadie; and he may have derived from him some suggestions toward his later concept of the *ecclesiola* or little church of true saints.

But the ingredients that entered into Spener's mental and spiritual equipment were many and varied. The influence of Stoll was continued for many years, and may have affected his stress upon the practical application of religion. At the University of Strasbourg, Johann Conrad Dannhauer had stressed Luther's theology. The young Spener was a diligent reader, and we know some of the books that impressed him. The German work of greatest value for him was John Arndt's *True Christianity,* published 1605–1609, before the Thirty Years' War. Arndt's aim was to induce theologians and lay people to turn from controversy to fellowship and charity, and from the confessions of faith to faith itself. He held it essential to add holiness of life to purity of doctrine. Arndt has passages that accord with salient ideas of Pietism. Take, for example, his teaching on the new birth. Man was created, he holds, to show forth the living image and similitude of the invisible God. By the fall of Adam he lost the heavenly image and became earthly and fleshly. A new birth is requisite for the restoration of the divine image:

" The new birth is the work of God, the Holy Spirit, whereby a man from a child of wrath and damnation becomes a child of blessedness, from a sinner righteous, through faith, Word, and sacrament; whereby, too, our heart, sense, and mind, understanding, will, and affection are renewed, enlightened, and made holy . . . a new creature in and according to Christ Jesus " (*Vom wahren Christentum*, I, v).

The discussions of repentance and faith are similarly in accord with Pietist viewpoints.

There was a mystical element in Arndt, but it was subdued. In the work of Jacob Böhme, mysticism was dominant; Spener studied his writings hopefully, but found them disorderly and uncongenial. It is not clear how far Spener was impressed by the religious poetry of Paul Gerhard (d. 1676), in which we find anticipations of the Pietist spirit. Nor do we know the degree of his indebtedness to the Dutch Pietism that preceded him, in which Willem Teelinck (d. 1629), Gisbert Voet (d. 1676), and Jodocus van Lodensteyn (d. 1677) are outstanding personalities. Ritschl calls Jodocus " the first Pietist." It is fair to say here that the Reformed Church in the Netherlands was considerably stirred by this movement before Spener's German Pietism appeared. But we should not, because this Dutch movement has been called Pietism, assume that it was identical with the German Pietism of Spener. By some, indeed, it has been rather identified with Puritanism, on the ground that, like Puritanism, it sought ecclesiastical reforms. It was, moreover, richly fertilized by early English Puritanism; Teelinck had lived in England, and Voet read Puritan books.

In August Lang's view, William Perkins so completely anticipated the Pietists that he may be called "the first Pietist." Since, for this author (*Puritanismus und Pietismus*), Perkins stood in a succession from Bucer, an English line of connection exists from Bucer to Spener. Whatever his relation to Perkins, there is no doubt of Spener's debt to other English writers. To some of these he was greatly attracted at an early age. Perhaps most influential was the oft-published and widely translated handbook of Lewis Bayly (or Baily), *The Practice of Pietie,* which first appeared about 1610 and was published in German at Zurich in 1629. Bayly was a Welsh minister of Scottish descent and of strongly Puritan opinions. Though he became bishop of Bangor (1616), he was later in trouble with Archbishop Laud for utterances on the Puritan side. *The Practice of Pietie* exhibits the presuppositions of Puritanism. It contains a series of devotional exercises for morning and evening use in families and in private; meditations on fasting and holy feasting and on the Holy Communion; a "prayer before taking physick," and a series of prayers and consolations for the sick and the dying. It is not now an especially impressive book, but its early popularity in about fifteen languages is attested.

Spener himself says that God in guiding him used the careful reading of books translated from the English, "namely, the *Golden Jewel* of Emanuel Sonthom[1] and the *Practice of Pietie,*" along with

---

[1] "Sonthom" or "Sonthomb" is supposed by Paul Grünberg (*Philipp Jakob Spener,* I, 131) to be an inversion of "Thompson"; but having sought among the approved bibliographical guides, I have so far failed to find an English writer of the name and time or any evidence that the book was ever printed in English. The *Guldenes Kleinod* appeared from a Strasbourg press in 1632. Spener says it was "often printed in Lutheran places and heartily beloved by many theologians" (*Theologisches Bedenken,* III, 347). It was reprinted in German more than once after Spener's death. August Lang (*Puritanismus und Pietismus,* p. 109) mistakenly identified it with the *Golden Chain* of William Perkins, a very different book. A copy of the 1632 edition is in the Library of the British Museum. The writer's aim is declared to be to show "how one who has the name of Christian may be a Christian in deed and in truth." The book is in three parts, and contains twenty-two chapters. Part I deals with the basic thoughts and motives that encourage improvement of life; Part II, with the hindrances thereto; Part III, with repentance and obedience. May it not have been translated from an unpublished English manuscript?

Arndt's book, and adds that he "rendered into German verse a chapter on the blessedness of believers" that had greatly stirred him in Bayly's book. In the latter the section referred to is entitled "Meditations on the State of a Christian Reconciled to God in Christ," and treats of the Christian's blessedness in life and death and the life to come. Spener later made use of Bayly's manual in his pastoral work. Other English authors used by him included the Puritans Daniel Dyke and Thomas Goodwin and the Anglican Joseph Hall, Bishop of Exeter and of Norwich.

Spener was also, during his pastorates, an appreciative reader of some works of Baxter in translation, notably the *Treatise on Self-denial* (1659), which appeared in German at Hamburg in 1665. It is a typically urgent admonition to a consecrated life, and contains much frank criticism of indolent and undevout clergy, such as Spener himself was to voice a few years later. Spener has several favorable references to this and other writings of Baxter in his late work, *Theologische Bedenken*.

II

We do not explain Pietism by citing the literature on which Spener was nourished. Yet he was a man who read in order to appropriate, and there is a real filiation of Pietism from both the irenical mysticism of Arndt and the practical devotion of Puritanism. Furthermore, his debt to predecessors was not confined to those of his own century. Spener had a penchant for history, and he read back through the centuries. He possessed a positive orientation toward medieval works of piety. He knew the teachings of the Reformation, and had the largeness of mind to view them in perspective. He felt himself nearer to Luther than to contemporary interpreters of Luther. He would honor Luther, but he regrets to say that "if Luther should rise again today he could not recognize as his disciples many of his spiritual descendants" (*Theologische Bedenken,* III, 84). He held that the Lutheran Reformation was left incomplete. "The departure from Babylon took place, indeed, but the temple and the city were not yet built," and there is needed now a fresh cleansing of abuses (III, 179, 180). Furthermore, Luther's authority is not final. He was a fallible man " far, far beneath the apostles." We must not follow him blindly; there is much in him that we must sorrowfully deplore (III, 712). While he remained critical of some points of Calvinism, he reacted against the anti-Calvinist animus of current Lutheran argumentation. It has been said that on his deathbed Spener confessed as a sin the uncharitable condemnation of the Reformed to which he had once or twice given utterance. The question of the influence of Martin Bucer of Strasbourg (d. 1551) upon Spener is an open one, but his whole view of the pastoral office resembles rather closely that of Bucer, and there is every reason to suppose that this is not accidental. Indeed, Bucer's emphasis upon the mutuality of the Christian life, and practice of " mutual edification " in group meetings at Strasbourg in the 1540's, may in some sense have furnished a model to Spener.

It was in Strasbourg that Spener began his pastoral labors (March 25, 1663). He accepted the call to Strasbourg, and ministerial ordination, with fear and trembling, and only after consulting his brother-in-law, Joachim Stoll, who replied, " The call comes from God." At his mother's prompting, Spener married Susanna Erhard, daughter of a prominent citizen, in May, 1664, and in June he was promoted to the doctorate in theology. In 1666, he was unwillingly released by the Strasbourgers to Frankfort, where he had a fruitful ministry of nineteen years (1666-1685). It was here that the Pietism of Spener, as a new movement affecting German Lutheranism, had its inception.

Spener, at thirty-one, placed over a group of pastors older than himself, and distressed by the prevailing irreligion of the people, courageously undertook a reform of religious instruction. In what was then a startling innovation, he broke from the limitations of the *Perikopen,* or appointed readings, and began preaching on texts of his own selection and on whole books of the Bible. He reintroduced the service of confirmation that had been abandoned, and set apart days of fasting and prayer. Still he felt that little was accomplished. The life of the careless Frankfort burghers remained unaffected. One day in 1670, he preached a challenging sermon on Matt. 5:20-26

("Except your righteousness shall exceed . . ."), insisting on the necessity of a complete conversion and a living faith. The response was surprising; it startled Spener himself into a fresh searching of his own conscience. Presently he was holding in his study group meetings of the awakened, using Bayly's book along with the New Testament; and a transformation of family life began to appear in the city. The *collegia pietatis,* groups of earnest folk meeting for study and prayer, constituted a notable feature of Pietism. But actually Spener found them difficult to maintain on a high level, and abandoned the effort.

In 1674, Spener was invited by a book firm in Frankfort to write an introduction to a new edition of Arndt's *True Christianity.* He did so, and the piece took the form of an independent treatise prefixed to Arndt's work, entitled *Pia desideria (Pious Longings).* This book has the importance of being the first formulation and manifesto of Pietism, and the date of its appearance, March 24, 1675, may be said to mark the end of the century of Lutheran scholasticism and the beginning of the era of Pietism. Some years later, to his annoyance, the name "Pietists" was applied to Spener's followers.

Pia desideria is a bold little book, mingling frank criticism with a program for bringing new vitality to the Church. The criticism comes first. Spener flays the upper classes and magistrates, charging them with worldliness and dissolute habits, and attacks their apparent assumption that government ought to be atheistic. He is dealing here, not with politics, but with the morals of politicians. He had early resolved to avoid political criticism. The sins of the *bourgeoisie* are reviewed; they include prodigality and drunkenness and a neglect of the works of charity. The clergy themselves are blameworthy; they are often scandalous and ignorant, and they prefer controversy to pastoral duty. The work of Luther, interrupted, must be resumed and the people lifted from their corruption, which Roman Catholics point to as the natural fruit of the Reformation.

The urgency, and something like the anger, of Luther himself is here. But Spener was no Luther. He was in reality an irenic soul, and most of all desired to be constructive. He argues that reform of these conditions is a possibility: And he proceeds to set forth what he regards as "the way to Reformation." Six requirements are stated:

1. The Word of God must be better made known through systematic public reading and interpretation, group study, and family and private devotional reading. In the group meetings (*Versammlungen*), all members should have freedom to express their ideas. These conferences would be a return to "the ancient apostolic sort of church gathering."

2. The restoration and active use of the spiritual priesthood. This Spener interprets (in agreement with Luther) as the offering by each believer of prayer, good works, and alms, not only for himself, but for others. Each Christian is to pray for all and care for the blessedness of all. This concept of a mutual cure of souls is a favorite one of Luther and Bucer, and not less of Calvin.

3. The people must be diligently taught that Christianity consists not in knowing but in action (*in der That*). The reference here is primarily to the implementation of love to our neighbor.

4. Controversies should be avoided or entered upon only prayerfully and dispassionately; those in error are to be met with heartfelt love.

5. A revolution in the training of ministers is demanded. The teachers must aim not only to impart knowledge but to have truth penetrate the soul. Spener recommends nonpolemical and edifying books, and finds his chief favorites of medieval vintage, such as the works of Tauler, the *Imitation of Christ,* and the *German Theology.*

6. Preaching should be so reformed as to be truly edifying; it should awaken faith and urge the fruits of faith, and it should be simple and free from learned ostentation.

In this mighty litle book Spener expressed the religious needs of his age with great effectiveness. He lived to write many others, all bearing some relation to this basic statement. Among these are *The Spiritual Priesthood* (1677) and *Impediments to Theological Study* (1690), obviously expansions of points 2 and 5 of the *Pia desideria.* The former consists of seventy questions and answers. The spiritual priesthood is defined as:

" The right which our Saviour, Jesus Christ, has won for all men and by which he saves his believing ones through his Holy Spirit, by virtue of which they bring acceptable sacrifices to God, pray for themselves and for others, and each one may, and ought to, edify himself and his neighbor."

Women exercise this priesthood, though not in the public assembly (60, 61); and it qualifies laymen to judge their preachers (70). In the treatment of the theological curriculum he argues strongly for practical studies to replace controversial theology. Here, and in his letters, he approves the liberal education that stresses language, history, and classical philosophy. In Spener a strain of liberalism mingles with the intensity of the devout life. In his *Nature and Grace,* a Latin work of 1687, he argues that grace is not wholly detached from nature or contrary to it:

" Thus in the very holiest works of grace, even those which are most directly prompted by the Holy Spirit, the force of nature is not utterly and absolutely excluded " (ii, 1–3).

Spener's influence was now spreading widely. He was praised and imitated, and he was unfairly attacked. One of his opponents, Balthazar Menzer, spread the charge that Spener was a Jesuit; another found him guilty of a heterodox insistence on the illumination of the Holy Spirit. The second assailant, Conrad Dilfeld, overcome in the end by Spener's charity, repented of his unjust charges. When Spener was called to be court preacher at Dresden, 1686, criticism and admiration alike increased. The movement was taken up at Leipzig University, where a group led by August Hermann Francke, calling itself *Collegium Philobiblicum,* met for prayer and Bible study. About this time (1689), Joachim Feller, professor of poetry at Leipzig, in a funeral poem digressed to define the new word " Pietist." A Pietist, he said, " is a man who studies the word of God and, taking it for his rule of faith and conduct, leads an exemplary life." But another professor, John Benedict Carpzov, a former admirer of Spener who had coveted the post he now held and had become an embittered critic, used the term in scorn as the name of a new sect, and aimed to drive the Pietists out of Leipzig. " Our mis-

sion as professors," said Carpzov, " is to make students more learned
and not more pious." (We may know campuses where the point of
view is familiar.) In March, 1690, the little fraternity of Bible lovers
was forbidden to meet again, and its leaders soon left the city. Two
years later Spener, who had been in difficulties at Dresden for having rebuked his pleasure-loving Saxon prince, John George III,
accepted the invitation of the Elector of Brandenburg (soon to be
King Frederick I of Prussia) to Berlin, and there, after a fruitful
but troubled pastorate, he died, February 6, 1705. His later writings
included the extensive miscellany, *Theologische Bedenken,* which
contains autobiographical materials in addition to theological interpretation.

III

We have mentioned the second great name in Pietism and it will
be useful here to become better acquainted with August Hermann
Francke, 1663-1727. He was born at Lübeck, but his father, a doctor
of law, removed to Gotha when August was a child of three, and
here he was well instructed until at the age of sixteen he was ready
for the university. He went to Erfurt, but very soon removed to
the University of Kiel, where he spent five years, and excelled in
Hebrew. He had exhibited in boyhood a religious seriousness but
had grown ambitious and religiously indifferent when the influence
of Pietism began to play upon him through Christian Korthold of
Kiel, an admirer of Spener. Francke became a *Privatdozent* at Leipzig in 1685, and soon afterward formed the *Collegium Philobiblicum,*
a Bible study group.

But Francke did not, like Spener and Zinzendorf, become devout
without a great inward struggle. He passed two years in deep concern and anxious doubt. He doubted the very existence of God, and
once prayed, " O God, if thou art, show thyself to me." " The more
I wanted to help myself," he says, " the deeper I was plunged in dis-
quiet and doubt." One day his boardinghouse master saw him with
a New Testament in his hand and remarked to him, " Yes, we have
a great treasure in this book." At the moment Francke's eyes were
on the words, " We have this treasure in earthen vessels," and he

was startled at the seemingly Providential coincidence. The account
he gives of this experience reminds us of the passages in which Scripture phrases startled John Bunyan in his time of anxiety, as vividly
described in *Grace Abounding*. The problem for Francke was more
intellectual. It centered in belief:

"I looked over my past life, as one looks from a lofty tower over an
entire city. At first I began counting my sins, but afterward I beheld their
fountainhead, unbelief, or rather false belief, with which until now I
had deceived myself."

Few men, perhaps, have been converted by their own preaching.
Yet a sermon of Francke's on John 20:31 ("But these are written,
that ye might believe . . .") marked the change from doubt and
depression to faith and comfort of soul. This was in 1687. The following year he visited Spener, residing with him for some months
at Dresden, and early in 1689 he returned to Leipzig to resume his
group meetings and to lecture in exegesis. But, as we have noted, he
and certain of his friends were obliged, because of their Pietism, to
leave the university. Next he had a pastorate at Erfurt, but this was
attended by conflict and ended in his abrupt expulsion. Spener, however, proved a friend in need to Francke; he induced the Elector of
Brandenburg in 1692 to invite him to the University of Halle, then
an infant institution just beginning to function. It was arranged that
Francke should draw his small salary from the parish of Glaucha,
whose pastor he became, but he lectured in the university, at first
without remuneration, and was made professor of Greek and Oriental languages.

Then began a decade of extraordinary achievement of a sort quite
without parallel in earlier Lutheranism. In 1701, Francke wrote a
chronicle of what had happened, and with his later additions it
appeared in English at Edinburgh (1727) as: *Pietas Hallensis, Or a
Public Demonstration of the Footsteps of a Divine Being Yet in the
World, in an Historical Narration of the Orphan House and Other
Charitable Institutions at Glaucha near Halle in Saxony*. The work
he here reports grew out of Francke's concern for the people of
Halle and its environs. He had compassion on the multitudes, the

teeming population of neglected folk, many of whom he found both destitute and demoralized. He began to assemble and catechize them and, as he says, distributed together "spiritual and temporal provisions." D. L. Moody used to say, "The reward of service is more service": Francke's responsibilities were multiplied as rapidly as he met them.

A school was begun for the destitute and neglected, but money was needed. Says Francke: "I bought an alms box, and this I caused to be handed about . . . to well-disposed students and all such as were willing to contribute." It is interesting to find that he hesitated to invite the rich, fearing, as he puts it, that they would refuse "to part with the smallest limb of their golden idol." Not much came in, and he soon took the modest course of keeping a box for contributions in his own much-frequented living room, with the text I John 3:17 inscribed upon it: "Whoso hath this world's goods. . . ." Not long after, he was elated to find in it four thalers and sixteen groschen, a sum of money equivalent perhaps to a ten-dollar bill. He later refers to this as the meal in the barrel and the oil in the cruse that did not fail. Some of the money was spent in hiring a poor student to teach children, and some for books — which were taken away by the young readers, and not returned.

Discouragement was lifted when Francke got five hundred crowns from an unnamed donor, 1695. He was prompt and inventive in his philanthropies, and every contribution was instantly put to use. Soon a whole series of institutions began to arise, on a shoestring plus Francke's faith in the providence and guidance of God. He began to support orphans, whom he placed in approved homes; then (1696) he purchased a house for a growing family of orphans. He aided poor students, but found them wasteful of their allowances and took a new step:

"I resolved in the name of God freely to board them instead. So I cast myself upon the providence of the Lord, hoping that his bounty from time to time would supply us with such relief as was sufficient for them."

He assessed the results favorably. The residence life was an improvement. It enabled him to study the disposition of each lad, and "to keep under stricter awe the whole tenor of their conversation," as well as to repel those who on pretense of poverty had accepted help, but were not willing to endure the austerity of the house. Soon he developed a large charity school, which had two sections for older and younger boys and two for girls, with four masters, and with books provided for use in the classrooms. Another school for fee-paying pupils, was instituted, but its work was integrated with that of the school for the poor. Classes were held in ecclesiastical Latin, Greek, Hebrew, history, and geography.

In Holland institutions of charity were far more advanced than in Germany, and Francke wished to profit by the Dutch examples. In 1697 he sent an emissary, Heinrich Neubauer, to Holland to investigate charity schools, and obtained useful information. He now purchased the tavern known as the Golden Eagle, and, to forestall the building of an alehouse next door, bought an adjacent lot as well; then he laid the foundation for a hospital, and waited upon God for money to build it. An architect advised stone, not wood, and stone it was. Men thought it would never be built. Said one, " If this wall comes to be finished, I'll hang myself on it." The building was occupied, Easter, 1701, but no hanging of the unbeliever is recorded. In 1677, the gymnasium, or Latin school, had its origin. It took care of talented boys, and soon attracted pupils from distant places and became a school of European importance. The *paedagogium,* begun with three pupils from well-to-do families in 1698, though much smaller than the Latin school, also obtained international significance. A House of Widows was established on a donation made in 1698; it had a garden, a chaplain, a physician, and a maid. It was designed, says Francke, not merely to support the poor widows but to instruct them in intercessory prayer for the city, the country and ruler, and the whole Church. He evidently had in mind the function of the enrolled widows in the Early Church (I Tim. 5:3-16).

Another tavern was acquired and transformed into a gynaeceum, a house for unmarried women who could pay for their support. There was a school to train students in catechizing, and (in 1704) a " Seminary of Preceptors," or teacher training institute. A young physician, Christian Friedrich Richter, turned over his property and gave his services, and with others established a medical dispensary. Provision was made for Halle students in theology to obtain some knowledge of medicine. A book depot was set up with the aid of another benefactor; it soon had branches in Berlin and elsewhere. A Bible house followed and was aided by a printing establishment under the Baron von Canstein, which produced Bibles cheaply in many languages, and much other religious literature.

Funds flowed in with every project. Many large gifts were anonymous. A timely shipment of thirteen and a half tons of herrings saved the faith of a downhearted steward. Clothing, tableware, jewelry, a share in a silver mine, beer, medicines were included in the miscellaneous gifts which Francke asked of heaven alone. He sent no anxious letters soliciting funds. His motive in writing *Pietas Hallensis* was not to appeal for money but to persuade the reader of the goodness of God. He states rather bluntly that he will place his trust in no contributor, but in God alone. In an appended section he writes as one who has lived in the center of a continuous miracle:

"For my part I readily confess that I have engaged in this affair, and am hardly able to give any sufficient reason for it. 'Twas I think a secret guidance of the Lord, whereby I was carried to the performance of such things as tended to an end I had not yet conceived in my mind."

The Halle Foundations grew out of the indomitable faith and creative genius of one consecrated man, with nothing of worldly calculation. Religion was always the primary concern of Francke, but religion brought with it an irresistible inner compulsion to assail what was evil and unsatisfactory in social life. He was no sociologist. Instead of making a study of juvenile delinquency, he combatted it with the agencies of religion. But as he observed the routine operation of these agencies, he saw clearly that they had a social significance. He was happy to give a service to the community as well as to the Church.

"Here [he writes] a foundation is laid for training up good workmen in all trades, good schoolmasters, good preachers and counselors, who of course hereafter will think themselves the more obliged to serve everyone because they have both an experimental knowledge of God's providence from their youth up and the benefit of a sound and solid education. . . . By such undertakings, therefore, the country will be cleared by degrees of stubborn beggars, thieves, murderers, highwaymen, footpads, and the whole pack of loose and debauched people " (p. 76).

Francke was the most distinguished promoter of Protestant foreign missions in his time, one hundred years before William Carey. In 1705 two young men from Halle, Bartholomew Ziegenbalg and Heinrich Plütschau, pupils of Francke, went at the request of Frederick IV of Denmark to Tranquebar, India. The successful mission that resulted was directed by Francke while he lived. As Pietism became identified with the cause of foreign missions, the Halle community became more ecumenical in its outlook. Yet Francke was somewhat narrow and angular in his theology. He was a constant and aggressive preacher and writer, and he did not escape criticism and controversy. He was more austere than Spener and less generous to opponents; his opinions were held with immovable conviction. His educational treatise *Short and Simple Instruction,* 1702, shows him very stern in his educational method: he does not favor children's play in any form. He preached against dancing, cardplaying, and the theater. Having been through an intense experience of conversion himself, he laid great stress on the new birth as a necessity for an effective ministry. His ablest opponent, Valentin Ernst Löscher, of Dresden, held that an unconverted minister may, if he is orthodox in his preaching, be an instrument of salvation to others, while the Halle theologians, Francke and his colleagues, Joachim Lange and Johann Daniel Herrnschmidt, assailed this view. A conference of the Halle men with Löscher in 1722 was marked by sharp antagonism, and was followed by the publication of the final section of an able anti-Pietist work by Löscher, *Timotheus Verinus,* 1718-1722.

Another issue was that of the confessional. Francke's old associate, J. K. Schade, who left Leipzig with him and joined Spener in Berlin, embarrassed Spener by a violent attack upon private confession as it was practiced in Lutheranism. Spener had his doubts about the

Lutheran maintenance of the confessional in its modified form, but he never desired its abolition. Francke found people neglecting the practice because they could not pay the *Beichtpfennig,* or fee for hearing confessions, and he substituted intimate conversations for the formal confession. In various ways, then, Pietism offered a disturbing challenge to the older Lutheranism. It expanded in an atmosphere of controversy more intense than we can easily imagine, and in Francke it possessed a convinced and somewhat dogmatic champion.

IV

We cannot now place on review the other Halle apostles and discuss the far from monotonously peaceable inner history of Pietism. But two other famous names must be mentioned in order to expand the range of our survey. Nicholas Ludwig Count von Zinzendorf (1700–1760) was a brilliant pupil at the Halle *paedagogium* from 1710 to 1716. A sensitive, precocious boy, he was greatly stimulated by Francke, in whose home he heard missionary newsletters read ("edifying reports of the Kingdom of Christ"). The program of the school, exacting as it was, was insufficient to capture all his energies, and at the age of fourteen he organized a boys' group, the "Slaves of Virtue" (later called "Order of the Grain of Mustard Seed"), whose members adopted a constitution in which they pledged themselves "to love the whole human race." He and his companions were stirred by the missionary interests of their seniors, and excited over the visits of Plütschau with a converted Indian (1713) and of Ziegenbalg, who was married at Halle to the sister of a friend of Zinzendorf when on furlough (1715).

But Zinzendorf had even earlier felt the attraction of Spener, who was his godfather and who, when he was four, had laid his aged hands benevolently on the boy's head and blessed him (1704). Zinzendorf was to have a dramatic career, and to exercise a wide influence. He was ardent, hot-tempered, and warmhearted, a man of impulse yet of earnest and unfaltering purpose. August Gottlieb Spangenberg, who lived on intimate terms with him for thirty years, testifies that he followed immutably "the purpose formed in

his childhood of serving the Lord with all his heart and strength."
His greatest achievement was the creation of the Moravian Church
from refugee fragments of Hussitism. Yet he was so far attached
to Lutheranism that he took holy orders in that Church. His relative
indifference to denominational peculiarities made it possible for
him to regard himself as a member of both communions. His statement (1741), "I can tie my testimony to no denomination," is out
of accord with the ordinary Pietist position.

After Francke's death (1727), his son and successor in Halle did
not find Zinzendorf satisfactory. In the reckoning of strict Halle
Pietists, the Count was an unconverted man. He had never been
other than a pious Christian since the age of four when Spener
had blessed him, and since he had learned to write and tossed out of
the window of his grandmother's castle notes addressed to Jesus.
His religious troubles at the age of nineteen and twenty were not
describable as conversion. Moreover, he had fallen for a short time
at Wittenberg under the instruction of men unfavorable to Pietism.
This led him, though only eighteen at the time, to propose an agreement between the orthodox Wittenbergers and the Halle Pietists.
As patron and bishop of the Moravians, he was now associated with
a non-Lutheran communion, while he still showed himself tolerant
of the orthodox opponents of the Pietists. It was not only at Halle
that he was regarded with suspicion and disfavor. He was widely
criticized for his extravagant mysticism and curious distortions of
doctrine, for his tolerance of Moravian usages, and for his utopian
projects of reunion with Roman Catholic and Greek Orthodox
Churches. He had far too much individuality and impatience to fall
into the mold of the Halle school and become merely a disciple of
Francke.

The Moravian Church, refounded by Zinzendorf, as it expanded
in Europe and America became a potent force in Christianity. It
was deeply affected by the peculiarities of Zinzendorf's Pietism. His
idea of the true Church as " the Church of God in the Spirit " made
him peculiarly free in denominational relationships. The Moravians
outside of the mother community of Herrnhut, constituted a " dias-
pora," testifying to their principles among other Christians. Zinzen-

dorf attempted to bring to unity the spiritual or awakened Christians
by the plan of the " tropes," or groups favorable to Moravian Pietism
within Lutheran, Reformed, or other Churches. In America this
was attempted in the midst of the German-speaking sects of Pennsylvania during and after Zinzendorf's visit in 1741–1742. The outcome
was not what Zinzendorf hoped for. The interpenetration of sects
did not lead to their unification, but occasioned increased suspicion
and bitterness. The validity of Zinzendorf's concept of a hidden
unity within all Christian communions ought not to be judged by
this outcome. There were unfavorable personality factors and other
adverse conditions. Zinzendorf was an apostle of amity and Christian
gentleness who was, nevertheless, inclined to be headstrong and
lordly. As the deliverer of the Moravian community at Herrnhut he
was permitted to be its master, but elsewhere he met resistance and
criticism. In America the most effective opposition came from Henry
Melchior Muhlenberg, a loyal representative and apostle of the
Halle school, who during the 1740's won the Pennsylvania Germans
to a sober, pietistic Lutheranism.

In the renewed Moravian Church the attempt was made to return
unreservedly to apostolic practice. This extended to the rites of foot
washing, love feasts, the kiss of peace, and the casting of lots. The
group life of the members was intensively cultivated, and residence
arrangements were made to conduce to this. " Choirs," or households
for persons of age groups, and " little societies," which were sub-
divisions of these, were formed and maintained. Common occu-
pations were attended by vocal and instrumental music, and occu-
pational hymns were employed (e.g., " Spin and weave compelled
by love, sew and wash with fervor "). Unfortunately this innocent
fervor of the Moravians was marred by a morbid devotion to the
wounds of Christ, which reached a stage of uninhibited and repulsive
extravagance. Many of the hymns used had erotic imagery of Christ
the Bridegroom mingled with realistic phrases descriptive of Christ's
agony and bloody sweat. These phenomena appeared both in Europe and in America. In the settlement of Herrnhut in the late
1740's, the followers of Zinzendorf called themselves (to select a
mild example) " little fools, children, virgins that were only to enjoy

themselves in the wounds of Jesus." Zinzendorf was himself the inspirer of these pious extravagances. Thereby he lost the admiration
of many well-wishers and gave opportunity to his defamers. Theo-
logically too he was wayward. His conception of the Trinity as Father, Mother, and Son was shocking to many. It has been pointed
out that this did not mean the subordination of the Son. Instead,
primary devotion was paid to Christ, who was said to be the Person
named in the clause, " Our Father which art in heaven." God the
Father receded into the background so as to become " a kind of
Grandfather " to believers.

Ultimately Zinzendorf responded to the censure he had incurred,
called in and burned many of his objectionable hymns, desisted
from the use of offensive theological phrases, and honestly repented
of his strange aberrations. The movement he had instituted came
under the control of August Gottlieb Spangenberg, a man endowed
with wisdom no less than piety, who led the Moravians on safer
paths. Because of his adherence to Zinzendorf, Spangenberg had for-
feited the good will of the Halle authorities in the days of Francke's
successor (1733).

Despite this severance, Zinzendorf must be regarded as a real Pietist. His personal devotion was of the Pietistic type, and his interest
in missions, vigorously expressed in the Moravian Church under his
influence, was initially aroused in the Halle circle.

V

A particularly attractive Pietist of Zinzendorf's generation was
John Albert Bengel (1687–1752), in whom the liberal Pietism of
Würtemberg had its greatest figure. At the University of Tübingen,
Bengel fell under the influence of Pietist teachers. He began to read
Spener and Francke, and spent a fruitful and very happy summer
(1713) at Halle. In a letter of June 17, 1713, he describes vividly the
studious and pious life of a Halle student, and comments admir-
ingly upon the lectures of Francke and his associates. From 1713 to
1741 Bengel was a distinguished teacher in the new seminary at
Denkendorf. He was a good classical scholar, and a lover of Cicero.

He edited Cicero's letters and certain treatises of Gregory Thaumaturgus and Chrysostom, but reserved his major effort for the study of the New Testament, in the textual knowledge of which he was unequaled. He made important contributions to the establishing of the Greek text, and in the field of exegesis. Bengel became somewhat celebrated for his saintliness, and was equally beloved by his students and by the ministers whose superintendent he became. He used simple rules of life, and recommended these to his students. Here are examples:

" Let your one object and endeavor in everything be the glory of God, a good conscience, and sincerity about becoming instrumental to the good of the public.

" Be careful to keep an accurate diary and memorandum book.

"Examine yourself from time to time, and especially at the close of each week, what progress you have made in everything."

Bengel was a pastor of pastors, and he wrote on pastoral problems with wisdom and insight. His correspondence contains much thoughtful and kindly admonition to ministers and lay people, sick and well. His letters and other writings attest the fact that (in contrast with Zinzendorf) he lived in great inward composure and was hardly capable of doing or saying anything ill-considered. Toward Zinzendorf's extravagances he could not but feel repulsion, but he was very patient with the zealous Count, and withheld his censures for many years. Finally he published some criticisms of Zinzendorf's " novel phraseology " and offered corrections of his New Testament translation. Bengel's biographer, J. C. F. Burk, connects Zinzendorf's repudiation of his censurable views with the gentle criticism he received from Bengel. If Bengel differed from Zinzendorf in his moderation and patience, he differed equally from Francke in the absence of legalism and the general liberality of his outlook. His six (surviving) children were successfully raised on a discipline that would have shocked Francke. Bengel wrote:

" If every opportunity for gross conduct is taken away, youth will do better kept to their own choice of innocent pursuits and pleasures than if kept under the dictation of others."

In Bengel the very Biblicism of Pietism led to scientific study of the Bible and contributed to the rise of criticism. In John Salomon Semler (d. 1793) we see even more markedly the same transition. Semler was not merely a textual but a historical critic. As the forerunners of the modern higher criticism began to appear, and to take comfort from his researches, the devout Semler felt much as some of the scientists who developed the atom bomb feel toward the product of their efforts, and voiced his perturbation and alarm.

VI

We see, then, that Pietists differed, and disagreed. Johann Jüngst-Stetin remarks that there is no " normal Pietism " and that there are no " normal Pietists." Spener was anxious to dissociate the fanatical and sectarian elements from the movement, and Francke was unsympathetic toward all wayward mysticism. Yet the insistence of the demand for dedication of life led those of less practical judgment to exaggerations of word and behavior.

There were many besides Zinzendorf who under Pietist influence indulged unwholesome emotions, enjoyed mystical revelations, and affirmed strange doctrines. Werner Marholz has edited personal records of a wide variety of types of experience among Pietists. One devout soul entertains quietistic notions of disinterested love, attains an unspeakable joy, and has visions in which he talks with Christ of heavenly things. Another goes into religious ecstasies, and enters on wide travels extending from England to Moscow. There are extraordinary conversions, as that of the anonymous diarist who was saved from death after being twenty-eight hours buried under stones and sand, and rose to newness of spiritual as well as physical life; or the very different case of one who happened on a tract of William Perkins and was plunged into inexpressible anxiety from which after two years he escaped, through reading other English books, with a flaming love of Christ. Some were melancholic. One of these mourns over his dead wife who, he fears, has joined the company of the wicked through his fault. He complains that his heart clings to the world, small though the reason be:

"O God, it knows thee not; it thinks on thee with thanklessness, indeed, with secret hate, as one who is condemned looks upon his judge. . . . Give me, O God, the grace to cling to thee with constant, earnest prayer."

Among the life histories of Pietist women, notable is that of Eleanore Petersen, who could not accept the doctrine of eternal damnation, and who received a revelation of the conversion of the Jews and heathen, in a bright and intricate dream, fascinating in its symbolism.

These are the common manifestations of intense religious excitement, and might be paralleled in other environments than that of German Pietism. When people are suddenly and deeply affected by religion, they often show symptoms of this kind, though their leaders may view such phenomena with some embarrassment. In the psychological realm there is indeed " no normal Pietism." In the realm of thought and books and co-operative effort, Pietism has, however, a recognizable character. We can offer here only broad judgments of it, with the attitudes and teachings of its greatest leaders chiefly in mind.

VII

Historians have generalized upon Pietism in various ways. Albrecht Ritschl thought of it as essentially a revival of medieval monasitc and mystical piety on the soil of Protestantism, stimulated from Reformed and Puritan sources and alien to the spirit of Lutheranism. Jüngst-Stetin, on the contrary, regards it as a progressive movement within Lutheranism. K. S. Pinson finds in it a psychological force that made for the rise of the national spirit in Germany.

We have seen some evidence of the influence of Puritan writers on the founder of Pietism. Many scholars have essayed to compare Pietism with Puritanism and some have regarded these movements as closely similar or virtually identical. The elements common to them have been brought to light by H. L. J. Heppe, A. Lang, and other historians, and what E. S. Waterhouse (in Hastings, *Encyclopaedia of Religion and Ethics*) speaks of as " a certain Puritan strain " in the Pietist pattern of conduct is beyond question. Ernst Troeltsch sees likenesses and differences, and points to the strengthening of Continental Pietism through the influence of Bunyan. Ralph Bronkema in *The Essence of Puritanism,* quoting many modern opinions, examines their relationships at some length and stresses the differences rather than the similarities. Pietism, he thinks, was more "individualistic and subjective" than Puritanism. Pietism was emotional, while Puritanism was "more stolid, austere, and in a sense intellectual." Pietism emphasized love and joy; Puritanism emphasized faith and works, and became somber. Pietism arose as a reaction against formalism, Puritanism as a reaction against Romanism and immorality. It must be said that in the course of his argument these generalizations are considerably modified. It is rather obvious that they require some correction. The Puritans also denounced formalism, while the greater Pietists were adamant against the papacy; and nobody could be more insistent on good works than Francke. And while Spener taught "heart religion," and gave recognition to emotion, there were likewise some Puritans who cultivated an intense religious emotion. They were alike in their emphasis upon a disciplined life and demand for practical training for ministers. Like Puritanism, Pietism was "intellectual" at least in the sense of possessing a concern for education and the training of the mind, and some Pietists were men of distinguished learning. The movement gave, indeed, an impulse to popular education in Germany comparable to that given by Puritanism and Nonconformity in England, and of greater relative importance. The Pietists first used the vernacular in university lectures, and they promoted the technical, vocational aspects of education in a most significant way.

The real differences are notable, however. One difference lies in the attitude to worship. Resemblances of Pietism to Puritanism here are accidental. The Puritans were in revolt against a formal liturgy cluttered with medieval accretions. Spener had far more to say in criticism of preaching than of worship, and his modifications of worship were slight. Another difference is that, while the Puritans took to politics like ducks to water, the Pietists — following an early personal decision of Spener — avoided political issues. The Lutheran ac-

ceptance of the political society as " given " and to be endured was
not challenged by Spener; and no doubt the environment offered
discouragement to voluntary political effort.

Despite Pietism's avoidance of politics, Dr. Pinson has discovered in it the sources of nineteenth century German nationalism.
His evidence is not very convincing. In this connection the importance he would have us give to the use by the Pietists, and later by
leaders of the national movement, of certain key words seems not
justified. It is doubtless true that Pietists talked a great deal of
Wiedergeburt (new birth) and that Fichte employed this word with
reference to the German nation. But it is unsafe to argue from such
data that Pietism was the matrix of German nationalism. There is
nothing to prevent a political party from helping itself to the vocabulary of religion. The Italian national *Risorgimento* (Resurrection)
was not dependent on a religious movement. Even the Pietist promotion of the educational use of the German language was not a
nationalistic phenomenon, but a means of securing the readier spread
of knowledge. Admittedly, it is also true that any movement in religion that stirs a whole nation, even though controversies may
attend it, helps to unify the nation's culture. Pietism did stir the
German people and, so to speak, awakened them out of moral and
religious sleep.

On the other hand, Germany has seen no movement more ecumenical in spirit than Pietism, more aware of the whole world and
concerned with the issues in world-wide Christianity. If it inadver-
tently in some degree aided later nationalism, it deliberately and
zealously inculcated an interest in the Church's far-extended fellowship and task. Pietism remained a distinct factor in German life,
with many manifestations, to the days of Schleiermacher, Jung-
Stilling, and the Baroness von Krüdener. It passed to Denmark,
Sweden, and Norway, and was infused into the rising Lutheranism
of America. It was influential in Switzerland, and it stimulated the
Methodists and Evangelicals in England and the founders of British
missionary societies. It reached out to New England Congregationalism and to the Reformed Churches of Germany, Holland, and
America. Whether it is in any sense a revival of a pre-Protestant pi-

ety or not, it has added something to Protestantism, something without which Protestantism would be vastly the poorer. The words of Cotton Mather, who was in correspondence with Francke, in his report of this interchange published as *Nuncia bona e terra longinqua* (1715), are appropriate here.

" The world begins to feel a warmth from the fire of God which thus flames in the heart of Germany, beginning to extend into many regions; the whole world will ere long be sensible of it."

THE EVANGELICAL MOVEMENT

I

The status of religion in human societies is never constant. In England and Scotland, a low point in the vigor of the churches and in the sincerity of the Christian profession was registered in the early eighteenth century. At the upper levels of society there was an emancipation from dogma, and widespread rejection of even the most elementary principles of Christianity. The influence of such books as John Toland's *Christianity Not Mysterious* (1696), Anthony Collins' *Discourse of Free Thinking* (1713), and Thomas Woolston's *Discourses* on the miracles (1727-1729) was such as to break down the traditional beliefs to which both Puritans and Anglicans of the previous century could confidently appeal. George Berkeley was among those who fought back vigorously, but until the appearance of Joseph Butler's *Analogy of Religion, Natural and Revealed* (1736), no very impressive systematic defense of Christianity against Deists and Freethinkers appeared. Bishop Butler hardly overstated the case when he wrote, "It has come to be taken for granted that Christianity is no longer a subject of inquiry, but that it has now at length been discovered to be fictitious."

Montesquieu on returning from a visit to England in 1731 expressed the opinion that there was "no such thing as religion there and the subject, if mentioned in society, excites nothing but laughter." The conditions that might lead a visitor to that conclusion are well attested. Profanity, inhumanity, and the grossest political corruption went unrestrained and almost unrebuked. Life for most was as unhappy as it was unholy — in the phrase used by Hobbes in another connection, it was "nasty, brutish, and short." The poorer classes were ignorant, drunken, and depraved. The laws were harsh, and men were executed for minor as well as major crimes. If life was cheap, so also was gin. It was consumed with such abandon that some charge to its effects the startling excess of deaths over births that is a feature of the early decades of the century. The gin evil was partly corrected by legislation of 1751: ten years earlier (1740–1742), the number of burials in London had doubled that of baptisms. The churches were ill attended, public worship was formal and spiritless, and the sermons generally reached only the level of platitudinous moral discourses in which Christianity was rather patronized than espoused.

In this unfavorable environment religion had, to be sure, its faithful professors; but they were a feeble flock. Anglicanism brought forth a series of " societies for the reformation of manners." These societies had grown fairly numerous by the end of the seventeenth century. Dr. Horneck, their chief originator, laid down such restrictions as that there should be no discussion of the government of Church or State, that no prayers should be used but those in the Prayer Book, and that the members must " shun unnecessary resort to taverns." While they were chiefly concerned with moral discipline, the religious interest was also strong. Among the Evangelicals the life of religion was to be cultivated with no such encumbering safeguards.

Nonconformity, which inherited the Puritan piety, showed some sparks only of vital religion. In its ranks Isaac Watts and Philip Doddridge stand out for their vigorous testimony to the claims, and the power, of Christianity. Although Watts was to furnish some of the hymnody of the Evangelical movement, his liberal theology would have rendered him uncomfortable with the typical Evangelicals of the later decades. Doddridge, however, would have been at home with most of them, and his *Rise and Progress of Religion in the Soul* (1744) was to be canonized in Evangelical piety. It was designed to awaken the irreligious and lead them to conversion. Although Doddridge praises certain Anglican writers of an earlier generation, his spiritual affinities are with the Puritans and he may be said to form a link between Puritanism and Evangelicalism.

The debt of the Evangelicals to the Puritans was, indeed, very great. They revived the emphasis seen in Bunyan and Baxter upon repentance and conversion, and inculcated the moral principles that Puritanism had stressed. Early Scottish Evangelicalism fed upon Thomas Boston's *Human Nature in Its Fourfold State*. This book presented a simplified Calvinism in the discussion of man in his " primitive integrity," " entire depravation," " begun recovery," and " consummate happiness or misery." Boston's thought had ripened under the influence of a Puritan book originally published in 1645 entitled:

The Marrow of Modern Divinity, Touching Both the Covenant of Works and the Covenant of Grace . . . in a Dialogue Betwixt Evangelista, *a Minister of the Gospel,* Nomista, *a Legalist,* Antinomista, *an Antinomian, and* Neophytus, *a Young Christian.* By E. F.

It was apparently the work of Edward Fisher, an Oxford graduate, the son of an English knight. Boston found the book in a cottage at Simprin in 1704, whither it had come in the knapsack of a soldier of Cromwell's army. It contained in dialogue form the teachings on grace of Luther, Calvin, Hooker, and other honored writers, and was designed to stress the invitation of the gospel, " Whosoever will, let him come." Here is a sample of Evangelista's exhortations to Neophytus:

" O, therefore, I beseech you stand no longer disputing; but be peremptory and resolute in your faith, and in casting yourself upon God in Christ for mercy, and let the issue be what it will. . . . God cannot find it in his heart to damn such an one."

The book proved a great illumination to Boston, and transformed his pulpit message. The " Marrow controversy " that followed the republication of Fisher's book in 1717 marks the clash of this evangelical Calvinism with the more rigid and scholastic Calvinism that had prevailed. Boston was opposed to Calvinist " neonomianism " much as Spener was opposed to Lutheran scholastic orthodoxy. The stress he laid upon " assurance " was greater than the older Calvinism in Scotland had ventured to affirm.

Ebenezer and Ralph Erskine were prominent in the small group of Boston's supporters, the " Marrow Men " as they were called. The Erskine brothers were to promote the Evangelical cause after Boston's death (1732), and were largely instrumental in the rise of the Scottish Evangelical movement. The Marrow Men, under investigation for heresy, declared *inter alia:*

" It is a great folly for any man to say — it may be I am not elected . . . therefore I will not accept of it nor come in . . . rather say, I do believe in Christ, and therefore I am sure I am elected. . . . Say then, I beseech you, with a firm faith, the righteousness of Jesus Christ belongs to all that believe."

It will be worth giving some further attention to the Erskines, and especially to Ebenezer, whose personal experience is of the Evangelical pattern. " In the summer of 1708," says A. R. MacEwen, in Erskine's own phrases, " he got his head out of time into eternity," and on August 26, God " brought his heart to give a consent unto Him." This consent to God took the form of a personal covenant, or dedication, such as Doddridge also made a few years later; and let us remember the not dissimilar act of Pascal in 1654. In this covenant Erskine uses the most solemn terms, and concludes: " I give myself away, in soul and body and estate, and all I am or have in this world, unto God, Father, Son, and Holy Ghost." In his personal prayer life, of which we get glimpses in his *Journal,* he craved that he " might be an instrument to build up a kingdom for Him among His people." " I had this day," he notes at one point, " a solid impression of God upon my spirit and of the great worth of precious souls."

Ralph Erskine was five years younger than Ebenezer. At Edinburgh University he had become a good Latinist, and he had fine gifts of expression in verse and prose. He was ebullient and humorous, and at the same time prayerful and conscientious. Ebenezer at Portmoak and Stirling and Ralph at Dunfermline alike imparted to their parishioners new spiritual life. Ebenezer's sermons (preserved by a corps of eager shorthand recorders) were admitted by an opponent to contain " the gospel in its majesty." By 1714 he was forced by increasing crowds of hearers to preach in a field adjacent to his church. He instituted " praying societies " in the various districts of his parish, a feature comparable to the *collegia pietatis* of Spener and to the classes later set up by Wesley. Ralph's sermons offer flights of imagination and illustrations from nature that link him with the literary romanticism then just beginning to appear, and he mingles spiritual feeling and symbolism with the plain offer of the gospel. They were not men of great austerity. Ralph took delight in his " wee, sinful fiddle," and wrote pleasant doggerel in praise of tobacco. Ebenezer had on his conscience at times his intemperate use of snuff. But they were not so free in their behavior as their brother-in-law, Rev. Alexander Webster, of Edinburgh, who was equally noted for his evangelical zeal and for his matchless capacity to consume alcohol without injury to his wit. The note of the gospel invitation was dominant in the pulpit doctrine of the Erskines, and mere anxiety about one's own predestination was held to be perverse and futile.

II

Doddridge, Boston, and the Erskines were the harbingers of the Evangelical movement. They were all Calvinists, as was their American contemporary Jonathan Edwards, who by 1726, having wrestled with doubt and Arminianism, could affirm that the doctrine of election was " exceeding comforting and sweet." Some light on the Calvinist character of this incipient Evangelicalism is cast, I believe, by an anonymous tract attributed to Sir Richard Farrington: *The Religion of Many of the Clergy of the Church of England Since the Reign of King James the First. By a Lover of Truth and Godliness.* London, 1707. This writer is convinced that the sad condition of the Church of England " in this time of degeneracy " is a result of the prevalence of Arminianism, which since it was embraced by Archbishop Laud has been adhered to by High-churchmen. They teach false notions of the mercy of God, derogatory to his holiness and justice; they " debase the glory of God's grace, and exalt pride in man." Neglect of the doctrine of perseverance in holiness on the

part of believers takes away the ground of their " comfort and joy."
The authoritative documents of Anglicanism form the basis of an
argument against these Arminian positions. Particularly striking is
the writer's lament:

" The work of conversion (which is the chief end of all preaching) hath
been at a stand. Where do we see that men are brought over from the
power of Satan unto God, are regenerated, and show the truth of their
regeneration by their evangelical obedience? "

The High-Church clergy, it is charged, use the word " schism " as a
theological scarecrow.

Boston and the Erskines had much the same feeling as this toward the Scottish Moderates. While this party had not yet become
dominant in the General Assembly of the Kirk, it had become influential in theological circles. Professor John Simson, of Glasgow,
introduced (c. 1714) views regarded as Arminian, and later (1726)
on the doctrine of the Trinity used phrases interpreted as " Arian."
Despite a recantation, he was dismissed from his chair (1729), but
subjected to no further censure. Boston was so dissatisfied with the
mildness of the sentence that he solemnly protested against it.

The conception that Arminianism could bring forth no fruit of
conversion, no rescue of men from the power of Satan, was to be
rudely challenged by the work of John Wesley, who for the first
time in England associated Arminian doctrines with a zeal for
souls. Wesley's Evangelical predecessors were stoutly opposed to Arminianism as productive of a spiritless and compromising type of
Christianity, without conversion and without repentance.

It would be possible, no doubt, to find in Puritan writers of the
seventeenth century virtually all the theological ideas and emphases
of the Calvinist Evangelicalism of the eighteenth. Similarly in Baxter, who was of no theological school but, as he said, a " mere Catholic," much may be discovered that anticipates the Evangelical
teaching of Wesley. What, then, is the distinctive character of the
Evangelical movement, and how is it related to Puritanism? Both
movements are of course complicated: each embraces a series of
movements; and Puritanism is the more complex of the two. It is

clear that Puritanism was much more concerned with political policies than Evangelicalism ever became. Evangelicalism resembles Pietism here; and Pietism was also one of its tributaries. It was not,
however, so purposefully detached from politics as Pietism, and
many of its leaders expressed their religious principles in political
causes.

The new element in Evangelicalism — and it was not new in any
absolute sense — consisted, I think, in the apostolic passion for the
regeneration of individual souls and the spread of sincere Christian
discipleship. The Evangelical felt the impulse recorded in I Cor.
9:16: "For necessity is laid upon me; yea, woe is unto me, if I
preach not the gospel! " In Erskine's phrase, "The great worth of
precious souls," was his controlling thought. Evangelicalism was not
primarily a reform of churches but an urgent presentation of the
gospel call to salvation. The negligent nominal Christian, the scoffer
at Christianity, and the heathen cherishing his idols were addressed
with equal urgency. It was not a defensive but an aggressive and
expansive movement, and its hunger for expansion was without
limit. If it leavened established churches and old denominations, it
was never content to operate within the hedges of one communion.
If it sought to mold the spirit of a nation, it was always ready to
carry its message to any nation and unto all the world. It actually
passed in succeeding waves over the entire Anglo-Saxon world, everywhere with manifestations of power. It called forth a series of
awakenings in many parts of Continental Europe and prompted
missions all over the globe. Most of what is significant in the Protestantism of the past two hundred years has either originated in or
been revived by the Evangelical Revival. It was not launched by
committees: it broke out in private experiences and meetings for
worship, surprising leaders and people; and it grew not only as a
campaign but as a contagion.

A new spiritual warmth attended the ministries of Boston, the
Erskines, and others, but the exciting stage of the Revival was en-
tered upon in the 1730's in America, Scotland, Wales, and England.
The first stir in America came, indeed, earlier, with the arrival at
Raritan, New Jersey, 1719, of Theodorus Jacobus Frelinghuysen, a

Dutch Reformed minister who had been selected as "an evangelical and pious man," and who with a disturbing passion preached repentance, conversion, and newness of life. Through Gilbert Tennent's association with Frelinghuysen (from 1726) the Revival spread to the Presbyterians of Pennsylvania, and a "spiritual hurricane" reached the flock of Jonathan Edwards at Northampton, Massachusetts, in 1735.

At just the same time, in Holy Week, 1735, a young man of twenty-one named Howel Harris (1714–1773) heard a sermon in the parish church of Talgarth, Brecon, South Wales, which moved him to make a devout preparation for holy Communion. First of all, he made peace with an offended neighbor. He spent months of anguish, however, before he found peace with God. He was induced to go to Oxford to be cured of his fanaticism. But he was unhappy in the unsympathetic environment of the university, and returned to Wales. He now began to exhort people, visiting from door to door, and opened a school. His exhortations became sermons, and were attended by increasing numbers. In the parish of Llangeitho, forty miles northwest of Talgarth, Daniel Rowlands (1713–1790), who was influenced by a dissenting Evangelical minister, Philip Pugh, was surprised to find his preaching becoming strangely effective. The emotional and physical phenomena of revivalism began to appear. During the litany the people not only cried out with tears the response, "Good Lord, deliver us," but some tumbled from their seats to the floor.

Harris became the chief itinerant apostle of the movement in Wales. He passed through strange experiences and was the victim of mob persecutions similar to those Wesley was soon to encounter; e.g.:

"At Newport the mob rushed on us with the utmost rage and fury. They tore both my coat sleeves, one quite off, and took away my peruke, I being now in the rain. *O sweet bareheadedness — under the reproach of Christ. . . .* Soon they halloed again and pelted me with apples and dirt, flinging stones in the utmost rage" (summer, 1740).

The adherents of Harris were often subjected to even greater violence than their leader. There were malicious reports and false charges.

Because they had meetings in the evening, it was charged that they put out their candles and had a " dark prayer " and other deeds of darkness.

It is remarkable that some historians refer to Wesley's conversion, 1738, as the beginning of the Evangelical movement. That event has an importance that ought not to be minimized; but the Erskines, Frelinghuysen, Edwards, Harris, Rowlands, and Whitefield had all begun earlier. The Welsh evangelists, with many lay exhorters, were stirring the people of Wales and organizing societies of the awakened before the new flame warmed Wesley's heart. By the end of his life Harris had been instrumental in founding about 300 of these groups. In 1751 he and Rowlands, in disagreement over the doctrine of the humiliation of Christ, parted company. He had a headquarters at Trevecca, where in 1752 a " household," dubbed a Protestant monastery, was established. It was a community of 120 or more, who had come there to enjoy the ministrations of Harris. Whitefield at various times co-operated with Harris. He had written to encourage him in 1738. In 1748 Lady Huntington established a seminary (School of the Prophets) there, and a year later Wesley visited the place. Fletcher of Madeley was made president of the college; but, owing to disagreements between Arminian Fletcher and Calvinist Harris, he soon resigned the office.

In Scotland the quiet pace of the revival under the Erskines was broken by the events of the secession from the Established Church, in 1733, and by other happenings. At Cambuslang, in 1742, under the ministry of William McCulloch, a strange earnestness on the part of the people appeared, and as he responded by constant preaching various evidences of revival followed. The awakening passed to other parishes; Kilsyth under James Robe, Kilmour Easter, Rosskeen and Nigg, were the scenes of similar phenomena. Ministers from Edinburgh and elsewhere joined in the spreading revival. George Whitefield had been with the Erskines the previous year, but they and the other members of the (Seceders) Associate Presbytery had failed in their effort to attach him exclusively to their group for work in Scotland. He now visited Cambuslang and witnessed, and by his preaching intensified, the excitement there. "It far outdid anything I ever saw in America," he wrote. "The people seem to be slain by scores." He preached to 20,000 at once, while the Erskines deplored the "Cambuslang Wark" as the effect of delusion. Nevertheless they did not wholly dissociate themselves from White-field, and the influence of Ralph Erskine upon Whitefield's theology is attested by the correspondence between them.

III

A conversion experience, decisive and dated, was characteristic of the apostles of Evangelicalism. George Whitefield gave for his conversion the date "seven weeks after Easter" in 1735; it was thus very soon after that of Harris. Whitefield afterward when in Ox-ford habitually visited the place where the change had come. He had much to celebrate, for he had been through prolonged agony of soul, marked by intense prayer and bodily mortifications, and had suddenly come to deliverance. He testified:

"But O! with what joy, joy unspeakable, even joy that was full of glory, was my soul filled when the weight of sin went off, and an abiding sense of the pardoning love of God, and a full assurance of faith, broke in upon my disconsolate soul."

He felt great gratitude to Charles Wesley for placing in his hands the book that chiefly brought him to this experience, Henry Scougal's *The Life of God in the Soul of Man* (1677). The author, a very gifted Scottish Episcopalian, had died at the age of twenty-eight in 1678. To John Wesley also this book was precious. It is one of the few books of the devout life that outlast the generations. A new American edition appeared in 1948.

Whitefield had entered upon the ministry with compunction and hesitancy, but his superb gifts as a preacher were soon in evidence, and, to quote his own language, he "began to grow a little popular." He possessed a speaking voice melodious and powerful. "I would give a hundred guineas if I could only say Oh! like Mr. Whitefield," said the actor, David Garrick. He is one of the orators of a bygone age of whose addresses we crave a recording. But in his case we should prefer that it be by television. The philosopher David Hume once heard from his lips these words:

"The attendant angel is about to leave us and ascend to heaven. Shall he ascend and not bear with him news of one sinner reclaimed from the error of his way?"

"And then," says Hume, "stamping with his foot, and lifting up his hands and eyes to heaven, he cried aloud":

"Stop, Gabriel, stop, ere you enter the sacred portals, and yet carry with you the tidings of one sinner being saved!"

Such forms of expression were natural to Whitefield. He had mastered the art of persuasion, and he had the courage to be dramatic. But Whitefield was more than orator and rhetorician; he was a mighty instrument for the transformation of lives. He added to his preaching many activities. In imitation of Francke, he established an orphanage at Bethesda, Georgia. He continually pursued his ministry by conversation and correspondence. Excessive labor apparently shortened his life. He died when on his seventh visit to America, September 30, 1770. Whitefield remained firmly Calvinistic in theology, wherein he diverged from Wesley. They ceased to co-operate in 1741, but were drawn together later on many occasions and held each other in the highest mutual respect.

John Newton, the son of a sea captain, became a godless, profane, and disreputable sailor, and the captain of a slave ship. After many strange adventures and bitter experiences, he turned to God and renounced his infidelity. "The Lord was pleased," he testified, "to vouchsafe to me peculiar mercy." Some months later, on an island off Sierra Leone, he was finally "delivered from the power and dominion of sin" (1748). He took orders and became the effective Evangelical minister of Olney, where his benevolent hospitality was supported by John Thornton, of Clapham, and where he was the friend of the poet William Cowper. He met here also Thomas Scott (d. 1831), who held a neighboring parish, and who for years regarded Newton and all Evangelicals with contempt, while he pursued his scholarly interests to the neglect of his people.

Scott later wrote a narrative of his own experience under the title *The Force of Truth.* Since it is one of the most informing documents of the Evangelical movement, we may here draw from its contents some materials relevant to our purpose.

Scott was so prejudiced against the " Methodists " (this word was applied to all Evangelicals) that he declaimed from the pulpit against them. When Newton visited two dying members of Scott's parish who had been neglected by their pastor, Scott awakened to his duties and began a correspondence with Newton (1775), still, he confesses concealing his true feelings of antipathy to him and trying subtly to draw him into theological controversy. Newton's invincible kindness finally broke down Scott's antagonism, and he became an admirer of Newton. He did not, however, look to Newton for theological light. Scott now began to examine his own motives. He felt grave scruples about subscription to the Thirty-nine Articles, since he did not believe the doctrine of coequal persons in the Trinity. He lost a preferment through these scruples — a heavy sacrifice, considering his growing family. Bishop Gilbert Burnet's celebrated book of guidance for ministers, *Pastoral Care,* led him now to reexamine the duties of the ministry, on which he had so thoughtlessly entered. Other helpful reading included Law's *Serious Call,* and especially the discourse on justification in Hooker's *Ecclesiastical Polity* — which contains, one may say, some unexpectedly Kierkegaardian reflections (" The little fruit we have of holiness, it is, God knoweth, corrupt and unsound "). Scott felt greatly drawn to Hooker's teaching, which he thought contemporaries misconceived. He turned to the Anglican *Book of Homilies,* and to his surprise perceived that the very doctrines he had despised as " methodistical " were the standard teachings of the Anglican Church. His preaching took on new emphases, and brought anxious, and embarrassing, inquiries from his hearers. He urged the perplexed to search the Scriptures, while he did so himself, and began a series of lectures on the Bible, for which he prepared with earnest study. He was now in candid quest for light, and as he read and pondered he became convinced of the Evangelical doctrine of the new birth. He began to have interviews with Newton, though still " ashamed to be detected in his company," and very loathe to be charged by his former friends with Methodistic enthusiasm. He then read unwillingly an essay of Henry Venn (on Luke 1:67–79), and was struck by these words:

"Abhor as much [as the blasphemy that the Gospel is an imposition] a fawning upon Christ from year to year in your closet, calling him there your Lord and God, and then coming out to consult the world how far they will allow you to obey his plain commands without saying you are a Methodist."

Scott found himself described here, and condemned. He writes of it with the conviction that the Holy Ghost spoke to him in Venn's words of rebuke:

"It came to my heart with such evidence, conviction, and demonstration, that it lifted me up above the world and produced that victory which faith alone can give."

Thereafter he was "not much troubled by being called an enthusiast or a Methodist."

Stage by stage Scott was led to affirm for himself the doctrines of the Calvinist Evangelicals. Studies in the Bible undertaken in connection with his personal ministry to inquirers, and the reading of an old standard work of Dutch Reformed theology, *The Economy of the Covenants* (1684) by Hermann Witsius, brought him finally to accept the doctrine of election. The Bible passages, he says, "would teach predestination, election, and final perseverance, in spite of all my twisting and expounding." Accordingly, about Christmas, 1777, he began to use these passages "for the consolation of poor, distressed, and fearful believers."

Thomas Scott's *Force of Truth* has been compared with Augustine's *Confessions*. It lacks Augustine's eloquence and mystical elevation, but, like Augustine, Scott was led by his strange spiritual pilgrimage to feel a kind of awe and lasting surprise over the evidence of the personal guidance of the Holy Spirit:

"I consider myself as a singular instance of a very unlikely person, in an uncommon manner, being led from one thing to another, to embrace a system of doctrine which he once heartily despised."

He was at the outset conditioned against the Evangelical beliefs and practices by strong prejudices and great intellectual pride, and also by ecclesiastical connections and self-interest. He carefully analyses the factors uppermost in his experience, emphasizing the sense of obligation to his people, the candid search of the Scriptures, and the effects of prayer. He was struck too by the fact that he had not been instructed by those to whose party he now attached himself. He comes out as an Evangelical first and a Calvinist second. He is not intolerant of those who differ from him on predestination; but he pleads against the indiscriminate use of "enthusiast" and "Methodist" as vilifying terms by persons as prejudiced as he once was.

Scott was to succeed Newton at Olney (1779) and to follow him later to London. His laborious *Commentary on the Bible* was his greatest contribution to the Evangelical cause. But his other writings were widely effective and his personal influence was also great. Cardinal Newman's first religious awakening, as he states in his *Apologia,* came from the reading of Thomas Scott. There were many who held Scott in grateful esteem for the same reason.

Anglican Evangelicalism flowered also in the mystical — and muscular — William Grimshaw (d. 1793), Vicar of Haworth, who was on good terms with Wesley and Whitefield; in William Romaine (d. 1795), for over thirty years in the Church of St. Andrew-by-the-Wardrobe, London; in Richard Cecil (d. 1810) of St. John's, Bedford Row; and in Charles Simeon (d. 1836), eminent Cambridge leader of the movement. Joseph Milner (d. 1797), Church historian, who professed to discover an Evangelical minority in the Christianity of every age, and his brother Isaac (d. 1820), a gifted mathematician, shining lights at Cambridge University, were also prominent in its ranks. A group, chiefly of well-to-do laymen, formed around Henry Venn (d. 1797), rector of Huddersfield, and his son John (d. 1813), rector of Clapham, was dubbed by the Anglican humorist Sydney Smith "the Clapham Sect." There was nothing sectarian about the Claphamites except their Evangelicalism and their devotion to good causes. Their names include John Thornton (d. 1790), whom G. M. Trevelyan calls "the earliest of the Evangelical magnates," and his son Henry (d. 1815), banker and author of a book of family prayers, men of wealth who were the financial angels of many philanthropies. Other Claphamites were Zachary Macaulay, who once took passage on the slave ship *Mary* to observe conditions (1795); Charles Grant, Scottish Highlander, chairman of the directors of the East India Company; and the great William Wilberforce (1759–1833), celebrated for his long years of distinguished effort, in and out of Parliament, to end the slave trade and liberate the slaves. His reading, at twenty-five, of Doddridge's *Rise and Progress* while on a tour with Isaac Milner was instrumental in his awakening. He came under the spiritual direction of John Newton, then in St. Mary, Woolnoth, London, and counseled also with John Thornton and Henry Venn. Wilberforce was transformed from a gay young blade into a devout Evangelical. He paused in his public labors to write *A Practical View of the Prevailing Religious System of Professed Christians in the Higher and Middle Classes . . . Contrasted with Real Christianity* (1797), a thoughtful and widely circulated book of Evangelical propaganda. Wilberforce's antislavery crusade is a thrilling tale; it is not to be thought of apart from his devout Evangelicalism. This religious urge set him also upon other high designs. He formed (1787) a society to combat immorality; he attacked Sabbathbreaking. He founded *The Christian Observer* (1801); he led in the foundation of the British and Foreign Bible Society (1804); he lent his aid to schools, Sunday schools, work for prisoners, and many good causes and needy persons.

Of the women prominent in the eighteenth century Evangelical movement, Selina, Countess of Huntingdon (d. 1791), who supported Whitefield and Howel Harris in the formation of the Welsh Methodist Church, and Hannah More (d. 1833), who labored to convert people of the aristocratic and prosperous classes, share an equal eminence. In 1799, Zachary Macaulay remarked that Hannah More while staying at the home of the bishop of London " has a duchess a day to convert." She was praised as a talented and witty writer, but with the growth of her piety she gave up writing plays, and seeing them, and devoted her gifts to religious persuasion. In 1825 she expressed " singular satisfaction " in " the increase of reli-

gion among the higher classes." She also sought to combat the
illiteracy and degradation of the poor by instituting "village
schools"; but she condemned proposals that higher education be
made available to the children of the working class. She was in full
sympathy with Wilberforce and the Claphamites on the slavery issue.

IV

The interest of the Claphamites in humane and charitable effort
was nothing alien to the Evangelical movement. At the same time
the Haldane brothers, Robert (d. 1842) and James Alexander (d.
1851), young Scottish gentlemen, of whom the elder, Robert, inherited considerable property, having gone to sea, were both converted
in 1794 in different harbors, and devoted their lives to the gospel
at home and abroad. James became a Congregationalist and later
(1808) a Baptist. Robert sought to found a mission in India but
was prevented by the policy of the East India Company. He had
schemes for the Christian education of Africans in Britain, and
other projects of evangelization. Napoleon's conquests gave him a
great interest in the Continent of Europe. In 1816 he was in Geneva,
where he drew many students from the influence of their rational-
istic professors. Voltaire had said that the Geneva of his time would
execrate Calvin not less than the pope. Robert Haldane was chiefly
influential in the institution of the Evangelical Awakening (*Réveil*)
in Geneva, and made converts of César Malan and Jean Henri
Merle d'Aubigné, students who became leaders of an evangelical
revival in the Reformed churches of Switzerland and France. Haldane made a similar effort at Montauban, and paid for the printing
and circulation of many thousands of French Bibles.

Robert Haldane had little influence in Scotland; but the Evangelicals in the Scottish Church became more vocal in the 1790's and
sought to institute a foreign mission. So far as the Kirk itself was
concerned, this was to come later. John Erskine (1721-1803), the
most influential of the Evangelicals of this period, remained a personal friend as well as the collaborator in Greyfriars Church, Edinburgh, of Principal James Robertson, chief of the opposing party

of the Moderates, whose personality had dominated the Assembly, 1763–1780. In a later generation the division of sentiment became intensified, leading to the disruption of 1843.

V

In pursuing the story of the Calvinist Evangelicals we have by-passed the greatest of all leaders of the Evangelical Revival. John Wesley, on a fair judgment, has no equal and no rival among them. It is probably safe to assume that to most readers of this book his apostolate is fairly well known. Wesley himself wrote so much, and gave utterance on so many matters of human interest, that the reading of his works is an education in the history of his times. None of the Evangelicals was more alive to the contemporary scene. Yet none of them was more a saint. Measured in terms of increasing devotion to the work that he regarded as laid upon him by God, and of loving care for the men, women, and children whom he aroused to the values of religion, he has a high niche among the saints of the Christian Church. In him sainthood appears, not in ascetic routines or formal works of mercy, but in a prompt and disciplined activity, ready to enter into every situation of opportunity or need, an activity of which, so to speak, the motor fuel was a burning love.

Wesley invites the tabulator of background data. He was vitally related to Anglicanism, Puritanism, and Pietism. He was a part of all that he had read, a man on whom individual books made a permanent impression. Even if he outgrew the *Imitation of Christ* and Law's *Serious Call,* they left a deposit in his spirit; and even if he criticized Luther, he knew himself permanently indebted to the great Reformer. His references to Henry Scougal's precious little book do not indicate that he outgrew that classic. Books by Lord Peter King and Bishop Edward Stillingfleet that he read in his forties guided the grave decision taken in his eighties to ordain to the ministry. Yet on the whole he was an eclectic reader, and his appreciations were critical appreciations. He may have owed more of his equipment to his mother than to any author, and through her to his Puritan grandfather, Samuel Annesley. When he went about to institute his "Christian Library" in 1748, he consulted Philip Doddridge, for whom (as well as for Watts) he had great respect; and, like Spener, he found help in Baxter. His contacts with the Moravians led to some knowledge of the work of Francke, and he made a highly selective use of Moravian elements in his early organizations.

Like others here noted, Wesley underwent a transforming experience, and it culminated at a point exactly marked as to place and time (May 24, 1738). Some questions have been raised regarding the importance of this experience for Wesley. At any rate, before it he was wretched and almost incapacitated with long anxiety; after it he was an integrated personality with an absorbing purpose to "spread Scriptural holiness"; and less than a year later he said in quiet realization of his function:

"I look upon all the world as my parish; thus far I mean, that in whatever part of it I am, I judge it meet, right, and my bounden duty to declare unto all that are willing to hear the glad tidings of salvation."

Beyond this spiritual release, his sense of call and visitation of power, Wesley's achievement was made possible by his genius for enlisting people's emotional responses and employing their energies in worth-while tasks. Love and zeal were matched with discipline and labor. In particular, Wesley provided, in bands and classes, a vigorous group activity, featuring what the Church Fathers, Reformers, and German Pietist leaders called "mutual edification" and "fraternal correction." In 1748 he stated in his *Plain Account of the People called Methodists:*

"We advised them: 'Strengthen you one another. Talk together as often as you can. And pray earnestly with and for one another, that you may endure to the end and be saved.'"

Wesley liked to affirm that he was "of no sect but of the Church of England." But the Church of England was not encouraging to its loyal apostle. It is fair to say that any Church would have found him an uncomfortable member. Institutions do not welcome disturbing variants from the accustomed norm and fashion. In time the movement broke the bounds of Anglicanism and went on as a separate communion. But Wesley's influence was not confined to this organization. It has always been vastly wider than the series of churches that sprang from his work. More than in his lifetime the world has indeed become his parish.

Wesley frequently, and clearly, described the principles on which his work rested. He once wrote:

"I have one point in view — to promote, as far as I am able, vital, practical religion, and by the grace of God to beget, preserve, and increase the life of God in the souls of men."

In an amplified entry in his *Journal,* September 13, 1739, he states his view of justification by faith alone and defines sanctification. He repudiates the assumption of others that sanctification is an outward matter of doing no harm and helping our neighbor: it is "an inward thing, namely, the life of God in the soul of man." This phrase is Henry Scougal's title. Scougal had stressed the idea in his first chapter that true religion is "an inward, free, and self-moving principle" (hence rightly understood as a "life"). He goes on to say, in a sentence that both Wesley and Chalmers may have pondered:

"The power and life of religion may better be expressed by actions than by words, because actions are more lively things and do better represent the inward principle whence they proceed."

There was in Wesley a seemingly easy promptness in bringing the inward principle, which was primary, to expression in corresponding actions.

Like Saint Francis and John Wyclif, Wesley was chiefly a messenger to the poor. He distrusted the rich and highborn, sometimes even when they professed religion, and admired the virtues of the poor. He has several statements of this sort:

"In most genteel religious people there is so strange a mixture that I have seldom much confidence in them. I love the poor; in many of them

I find pure, genuine grace unmixed with paint, folly, and affectation "
(letter to Dorothy Furly, September 25, 1757).

After an agreeable visit to a pious home of the nobility, he wrote
in his *Journal,* November 17, 1759:

" It is well a few rich and noble are called. O that God would increase
their number! But I should rejoice (were it the will of God) if it were
done by the ministry of others. If I might choose, I should still (as I
have done hitherto) preach the gospel to the poor."

Wesley's ministry was to the poor and neglected folk, whose condition was England's disgrace. They constituted a large proportion of
the population, and from them he recruited a great multitude of
converts. Under the Methodist discipline they shed their poverty
and ignorance. The worldliness that now assailed his followers with
their prosperity became a grave problem for Wesley. He was baffled
by the results of the thrift that he felt was a natural fruit of true
religion. For this he devised a good formula: "Gain, save, and give
all you can." If you do not give all you can after you have gained
and saved, your prospects of salvation are those of Judas Iscariot.
But it was easier to teach people to " gain " and " save " than to
" give." His approval still went to the really poor. He wrote to Free-
born Garrettson in America, September 30, 1788:

" Most of those in England who have riches love money — even the
Methodists, at least those who are called so. The poor are the Christians.
I am quite out of conceit with almost all those who have this world's
goods."

Wesley was the only eminent Evangelical leader of his time who
was an Arminian in theology. He reacted strongly against the Calvinist doctrine of predestination, and republished Bunyan's *Holy
War* " disemboweled " of its predestinarianism. He wrote to Walter
Churchey, December 23, 1773: " I do not profess any coalition with
Calvinism. I see the mischievousness of it more and more "; and he
once wonderingly asked his Swiss ex-Calvinist associate, John William Fletcher (March 22, 1775): " What are the charms of Calvinism? . . . How is it that so many fall in love with her? " Yet there

is much common ground between him and Calvin — a statement that is also true of his master Arminius — and his ethical teaching can hardly be distinguished from that of Puritan writers of the previous century. There is the same intensity of discipline, the same austere budgeting of time, the same view of economic duty, essentially the same cautious treatment of recreation (in Wesley's vocabulary usually "diversions"). With respect to the last named he notes in a late sermon, on I Cor. 12:31 (1787), that brutal sports are going out of practice. He lists bearbaiting among these "foul remains of Gothic barbarity." He is not absolutely opposed to the tragic drama; though he himself cannot attend plays with a clear conscience, "possibly others can." Cardplaying too he will leave to the individual conscience. But he suggests various less questionable "diversions," such as planting trees, music, experiments, visiting the sick, and, above all, prayer.

With all his concern for discipline and good works, the heart of Wesley's mesage was a fresh presentation of the gospel as joyful tidings of salvation, by the free grace of God, offered to all, and flowing from inexhaustible love:

"This love we believe to be the medicine of life, the never-failing remedy for all the evils of a disordered world, for all the miseries and woes of men" (*Earnest Appeal,* 1743).

To our generation this may seem too simple. Yet some very sophisticated philosophers have come to recognize the primary importance of love, and our fatal lack of it in world society today. Wesley was not the man to exclude thought and planning and co-ordinated action. But he believed that the energy for the combat against "the evils of a disordered world" could be supplied only by an appropriation of the divine redemptive love: and in this he was as wise as he was religious.

VI

During the first half of the nineteenth century, Evangelicalism in Britain had two outstanding leaders, Charles Simeon (d. 1836)

and Thomas Chalmers (d. 1847). True to the type, each had passed
through a conversion experience following a period of deep concern. Simeon related that at Easter, 1779, "peace and abundance
filled his soul," while Chalmers in 1808 finally found himself
wholly committed to be "an ambassador of Christ." More than
most Evangelicals, both these men were concerned for the good
of the Church as an institution. Simeon was criticized by some
Evangelicals for his frank and sincere devotion to the Anglican
Articles and *The Book of Common Prayer.* Yet he held this loyalty
without bigotry, and did not hesitate to go on an informal preaching
tour with the Haldanes in Scotland. He was most of all an impressive
Scriptural preacher. He exercised a wide and deep personal influence
among young clergymen, and he helped to awaken the foreign missionary interest in Anglicanism. The heroic missionary Henry
Martyn was one of his disciples. All the intellectual activities of
Simeon centered in the study of the Bible, on which he wrote a complete commentary for preachers.

Chalmers had somewhat broader interests. He had early devoted
his talents to mathematics, astronomy, and philosophy, and was
later an innovator in establishing agencies to combat city poverty
and degradation. Although he led the party of the Disruption of
1843, it was not through the adoption of the principle of separation
of the Kirk from the State but as a desperate remedy against abuses
that had come to be associated with this relationship. He had earlier
written, with England in mind, a defense of endowments for religion. But he would suffer no restraint upon the functioning of the
gospel in the Church, no infringement of what he called "the spiritual liberties of the people." The Evangelicalism of Scotland from the
Erskines to Chalmers contended for the freedom of the parishes
and courts of the Church from secular dictation. In this attitude,
though in little else, they were on common ground with the founders
of the Oxford Movement. Chalmers employed in his sermons much
illustrative material from astronomy, and engaged in philosophical
argumentation of a sort shunned by most Evangelicals; yet the convictions that underlie his preaching are those of the Evangelical
school. His eloquence was sometimes pompous, but often urgent

with invitation and warning. No one could more forcibly expose
the self-deceptions in which we naturally take refuge from duty,
and no prophet was bolder in rebuking the rich for their injustice
toward the poor. The Bible was always interpreted by Chalmers as
making demands upon conscience and calling for social action. " The
benevolence of the gospel lies in actions," he declared (1813), not in
" the luxury of feeling. . . . You must go to the poor man's bed.
You must lend your hand."

In course of the nineteenth century, Evangelicalism within Anglicanism came to form a party defending a platform, rather than
a fellowship of apostles and missioners. This is usually associated
with the effects of the Tractarian Movement which treated the Evangelicals with contempt (as " the peculiars "). They were taken off
balance, shocked, and surprised. They were now associated, and
tended to be identified, with the Low Church party, and they no
longer played the aggressive role of former days. Apart from the
founding of theological colleges and the support of missions, they
expended their energies in combating Tractarianism, often in the
courts of law. They were also weakened by the rise of Biblical
criticism and of Darwinianism. The great successor of Wilberforce
in the party was the (seventh) Earl of Shaftesbury (d. 1885), author
of remedial social legislation and worker among the poor of London.
But Shaftesbury deplored the decay of the Evangelicals, and re-
proached them for their disunion and insincerity.

Meanwhile new forces of evangelization were becoming active in
many areas. Revivals took place locally from time to time in Scottish
parishes during the early decades of the nineteenth century, especially in the Highlands and Islands, where numerous eloquent
preachers aroused Evangelical fervor. From 1858, a wave of revivalism from America spread over Britain and northern Ireland. The
Scottish churches became more and more Evangelical in temper,
while they were also feeling the influence of the new critical scholarship. Professors as well as ministers were well-disposed toward the
religious awakenings. Some of Dwight L. Moody's supporters in
America were surprised and embarrassed by the readiness of the
eminent critical scholar George Adam Smith, when in America in

1899, to fraternize with their leader. British Evangelicalism welcomed and profited by the visits to England and Scotland of Moody and his singing colaborer, Ira D. Sankey, 1872–1885. Moody's simple and powerful call to discipleship, expressed in defective syntax, was heard with eagerness not only in great metropolitan assemblies but in the centers of British learning; and it produced amazing fruit in redirected and dedicated lives. His meetings were scenes of intense but not, as in earlier revivals, vociferous emotion. The impressions made upon many observers were those of astonishment; and recent historians of the era testify to the lasting effect of Moody's work. Many leading figures in the British churches during the subsequent half century were recruited to the service of religion, or invigorated for it, through response to his teaching and appeal. One of those who caught the flame from Moody was Henry Drummond (d. 1897), who exercised a persuasive ministry to students throughout the English-speaking world and by his writings reached a very wide public.

By his *Natural Law in the Spiritual World* (1883), Drummond helped many Evangelicals to a tentative solution of the dilemma of faith and science which had become acute for them as a sequel to the work of Darwin. Evangelicalism had taken the Bible as historically accurate and verbally inspired, and now both science and criticism assailed this position. In the outcome there arose a group of "liberal Evangelicals" who made terms with the new knowledge while others combated it on the authority of Scripture. In America the latter position was known as "Fundamentalism," from the book *The Fundamentals, a Testimony to Truth* (1910), which expounded five "fundamental" doctrines, including the inerrancy of Scripture. In England a new generation of Evangelicals began a series of activities about 1905, led by Guy Warman, later bishop of Truro; F. T. Woods, later bishop of Winchester; and others. They organized (1907) the "Group Brotherhood," which functioned through conferences and literature, and with changed leadership after World War I clarified the liberal Evangelical position. Important here was the conference at Coleshill in June, 1923, which resulted in the formation of the "Anglican Evangelical Group

Movement," to assert the convictions of the old Evangelicals " in the light of current thought." The conference declared:

" We confidently assert our continuity with the Evangelical tradition of the past, among the treasured principles of which we would emphasize the following: the eternal good tidings of the intimate and immediate relation of the believer to God through the redemption of the Lord Jesus Christ and the power of the Holy Spirit; the unique authority of the Bible; the high value of the sacrament spiritually interpreted; the passion to win individual souls for Christ, whether in the parishes at home or in the mission field abroad " (Leonard Elliott-Binns, *The Evangelical Movement in the English Church*, pp. 72 f. New York, 1928).

VII

The Evangelical movement has been characterized by an ecumenical spirit. Denominational traditions and confessional standards have not been allowed to hinder its adherents from sharing in common tasks; and it has always held in mind the world-wide character of Christianity and freely overleaped national borders. It gave birth to the missionary societies and enterprises of modern Protestantism: Carey, Duff, Martyn, Judson, and their fellows were its children. At the foundation of the London Missionary Society, 1795, David Bogue optimistically proclaimed "the funeral of bigotry." Evangelical missions, at any rate, have had a tendency to combat bigoted denominationalism. In 1845 the Evangelical Alliance was formed: a means of intercourse and, within cautiously prescribed limits, of unofficial common action, for many denominations. Its first world conference (London, 1846) was marked by great expectations of Protestant co-ordination. " The divine inspiration, authority, and sufficiency of Holy Scripture " was the first of its nine articles of belief. It played an important role for more than half a century, and helped to prepare the way for the broader ecumenicity of our day. The Student Volunteer Movement was born of Moody's work (1886) and led by John R. Mott, who also helped to promote the World's Student Christian Federation (1895).

The Evangelical movement has been subjected to much criticism, just and unjust. The "Methodists" in the eighteenth century were satirized by a score of third-rate versifiers. Some of these belonged to "hell-fire clubs" of blatant and blasphemous atheists. They represented the preachers as hypocrites and impostors. Hoxie Neale Fairchild (*Religious Trends in English Poetry,* Vol. II, New York, 1942), discussing this literary attack, remarks that the apostles of Evangelicalism were "greeted by a loud chorus of uncomprehending mockery." His evidence shows that the mockery was seasoned with lies and hatred. Some of the more discreet mockers were clergymen: of these the cleverest and most celebrated was Sydney Smith, who lived to turn his arrows upon the Tractarians. But the Evangelicals were far too obviously sincere and devoted men to be easily laughed out of court, and this type of attack seems to have had little effect. They were open to criticism, however, for a number of characteristic weaknesses and limitations.

Like the Halle Pietists, they tended to lay primary emphasis upon the experience of conversion. While they taught a high doctrine of Scripture, they laid undue stress on a limited range of Scripture passages that offered suggestions for discourses on conversion. It is generally agreed that as a group they lacked depth of scholarship and breadth of reading, and showed little evidence of intellectual power or originality in any field. With a narrow theology, they were not equipped to deal with the nineteenth century surprises of thought presented by the Darwinian view of human origins and the critical study of the Bible. They lacked distinction as writers: no Bunyan or Milton appeared in their ranks, and their books were largely edifying and hortatory tracts on a low literary level. This is no doubt largely a result of their intense preoccupation with practical service and direct persuasion. Scholarship and a writing style require apportionments of time not available in the Evangelical's crowded schedule.

With all the social achievements of Evangelicalism, its basic individualism was not always checked by a social interest. Luther and Wesley had rejoiced to find the grace of Christ as something "for me," and these two words recur often in Evangelical song. The better Evangelicals moved on from this experience rapt in a profound

10559

gratitude that could only find expression in service for others; but there was always the possibility of stopping short of this in a gloating assurance of a privileged status. William Cowper expressed the simple aspiration:

> " For me a blood-bought free reward,
> A golden harp for me."

Cowper had psychopathic symptoms, and, in his case, the hope often grew faint and dim. He could describe himself as a storm-driven ship:

> " Me, howling blasts drive devious, tempest tost,
> Sails ripped, seams opening wide, and compass lost."

But the former lines indicate a realm of dubious motivation in some of the more robust or egotistic Evangelicals. The same defect is apparent too in the vocational and economic outlook of some. In Doddridge's *Rise and Progress* (xxi, 4) there is a warning against the economic carelessness that will induce bankruptcy:

" Guard therefore, I beseech you, against anything which might tend that way, especially by diligence in business and by prudence and frugality in expense, which, by the divine blessing, may have a very happy influence to make your affairs prosperous, your health vigorous, and your mind easy."

Wesley expelled from his societies bankrupts who could not show good excuses. As we saw, Wesley found the discipline of his classes making " affairs prosperous " for the Methodists, and anxiously sought to arouse them to the peril entailed in this. But the temptation to worldly smugness has often caught up with those who have learned thrift in the school of religion!

Many of the Evangelicals too exhibited a ruthless severity in amputating from the body of life diversions and pleasures, and excluding from education the seeking of artistic and musical skill; in this they went far beyond the position of typical Puritans. On the other hand, many have been amused at the bright optimism of the Evangelical mind in facing the tasks of religion. In every generation it has hopefully projected the rapid winning of the world to the sway of Christ. Wesley exhibits this attitude in his sermon " On the General Spread of the Gospel":

" From Oxford where it first appeared the little leaven spread wider and wider. . . . It spread to North Britain and Ireland, and a few years after into New York, Pennsylvania, and many other provinces in America, even as high as Newfoundland and Nova Scotia. . . . Is it not then highly probable that God will carry on his work in the same manner as he has begun? "

The same spirit in a later day was expressed by the slogan, " The evangelization of the world in this generation." But if this betrays overoptimism, and a failure to appreciate the strength of the antagonist, shall we not also say that there is here a noble grandeur of conception that can hardly fail to challenge generations to come?

In justice we must recognize limitations and defects in Evangelicalism as a historical expression of Christianity. These do not cancel its vast significance for modern churches and the modern world. The identification of the churches with the tasks of social betterment, and the world mission that has laid the foundation of a Christian Church in the far continents and islands, constitute highly significant elements in the total situation of today, and they are in a very large degree the fruits of this movement.

Inevitably the methods, the theology, and the ethics of Evangelicalism must yield to changes. Its old forms are outworn. But no Christianity that departs wholly from Evangelical ideals will win the battle in this or any future generation. We ought not lightly to cast away its basic conceptions of the Christian task. We need to guard its sense of the importance of the inner transformation of individual lives, along with its emphasis upon socially remedial activity, and readiness to seize the initiative. The Evangelicals had more courage than prudence, which is better than having more prudence than courage. Even excessive optimism is ridiculous only where it is not accompanied by heroic effort, and of this there was no lack. There has been, in fact, a closer relation between hope and achievement in the projects of Evangelicalism than in those of most other religious or secular movements. We are in danger of exchanging its confidence and hopefulness for theological puzzlement and pusillanimous defeatism. Perhaps this is because we have not read fully enough the history of the past two centuries, but confined our outlook too much to our own era of frustration and tragedy. Christianity, to be convincing — nay, to be genuine — must be presented as joyful tidings, and as an invitation to souls undone to share in a new life. It is not effective when it is expounded either as a law or as a paradox. Its spokesmen must be able, like Wesley, " to declare unto all that are willing to hear the glad tidings of salvation."

TRACTARIANISM AND ANGLO-CATHOLICISM

I

Anglicanism in the early nineteenth century exhibited the plight of a Church that had long been under the unwholesome control of secular government. The promise of Magna Charta " that the English Church shall be free and have her rights entire and her liberties inviolate " had not been fulfilled. There were some medieval churchmen who desired the Church's autonomy, but actually it fared ill between the contending jurisdictions of king and pope. Between 1350 and 1570 the papal cause was lost and the royal mastery of the Church was established. Parliament seized control of the Church in 1640 and attempted its complete reconstruction. At the Restoration it recovered its former outlines and became once more the king's Church, but the Revolution of 1688–1689 left it in an unsatisfactory relation to king and parliament. Numerous acts of Parliament affected its status and ministry. Whatever power prevailed, the Church of England was imprisoned in an Erastian system, and, so to speak, beaten almost to unconsciousness by the secular state. In this it shared the fate of Gallican, Lutheran, and Reformed Churches in the age of the enlightened despots, though with its own peculiar marks of ignominy. After 1718, the convocations that had retained some fading dignity from a not inglorious past, but had become contentious and feeble, were discontinued except for *pro forma* meetings held (as Edmund Burke wrote in 1777) for the purpose of " making some polite ecclesiastical compliments to the king." The result was to deprive the Church of its primary organ of corporate utterance and action. Good men resented this repression, but dispersedly and ineffectively. Boswell tells how Samuel Johnson once broke forth angrily: " Shall the Presbyterian Kirk of Scotland have its General Assembly and the Church of England be denied its Convocations? " But the eighteenth century saw no rigorous affirmation of its corporate rights. The very principle implied in Johnson's indignant question seemed largely forgotten.

It was the enfeeblement of the Church as a corporate institution that rendered it unable to deal with the opportunities and perils of the Evangelical movement. The spiritual regeneration which this movement produced in individuals and sections of communities did not affect the Church as a whole. It is scarcely an exaggeration to say that there was no " whole " that could have been affected. To many minds the Church consisted essentially of amassed ecclesiastical properties that were utilized to support men in holy orders but were under no unified control. Above this it was for many the conveyor of baptism, and of certain formal ministries, and the custodian of a set of doctrines no longer vividly believed but not to be called in question. It was favorably viewed as a useful instrumentality in government, a makeweight against social change and the fruits of enthusiasm and nonconformity.

Bishops and ministers were appointed under a long-established system of patronage that was highly conducive to the ecclesiastical success of the spiritually unfit. The landed aristocracy and gentry clung to their inherited rights of patronage, and younger sons, not otherwise provided for, might expect opportunities from benefices in the gift of the family. If, however, they were unfit for, or disinclined to perform, clerical duties, they could satisfy the requirements by providing, at a low income, a curate, a man of less fortunate family position and often of questionable education, whose chief tie to his parishioners was the common bond of poverty. The nominal incumbent was thus freed from spiritual duties, and employed the incomes of the parish with notorious irresponsibility. Non-residence in some areas reached almost incredible proportions, and in some parishes the reckless holder of the benefice failed even to provide a curate in his habitual absence. Hannah More found in the neighborhood of Wells a group of thirteen adjoining parishes with no resident minister.

George Crabbe (1754–1832), from experience and observation as a rector in parishes of Suffolk and Leicestershire, described his fellow priests in verse in *The Parish Register* (1807) and in *The Borough* (1810). Crabbe is a kindly observer rather than either reformer or satirist; yet satirical elements enter into his gentle characterizations, and are the more convincing because free from invective. The closing section of *The Parish Register* introduces the aged sexton, " old Dibble," and recites Dibble's description of the five incumbents whose remains he has interred. There was " Master Addle," impressive while he paced the hallowed aisles with his sevenfold surplice over his ample frame, but dozing in the pulpit, where finally he passed away in slumber. Then followed " Parson Peele," who preached from the text, " I will not spare you," and in his exactions practiced what he preached. " Doctor Grandspear," on the other hand, was liberal and rich, and loved to feast his friends and to give away halfworn clothing. The " author rector " who followed is Crabbe himself, who shunned conversation with his people (though he had a liking for vagabonds), was careless of the vestments and devoted to study. The youth from Cambridge who ends the list is a hot Evangelical whose ardor burns out his weak body and leaves him a victim of consumption.

The Borough is in twenty-four parts, called " letters," of which only the second, on the vicar and the curate, is of special interest for us. Crabbe's description of the vicar is that of a Laodicean churchman, indolent, pusillanimous, and studiously inoffensive:

> " Now rests our vicar. They who knew him best
> Proclaim his life t'have been entirely — rest.
> His constant care was, no man to offend . . .
> Fear was his ruling passion."

He condemns no sin except that of innovation:

> " All things new
> He deemed superfluous, useless, or untrue."

Yet he has won the approval of his parishioners — the rich, the poor, the serious — and even of the Dissenters, with whom he has carefully avoided conflict. The curate is a scholar whose life is crushed by poverty. He lives in a poor hut with a sick wife and nine children, and with pathetic eagerness labors to produce a book.

In plain prose other clergymen of the day supply us with more damaging evidence. Charles B. Tayler (1797–1875), rector of Otley, in *Facts in a Clergyman's Life,* which though published in 1849 reflects experiences of the pre-Tractarian period, describes the grossly inadequate preparation of the ordinand who gets by the examination of the bishop's chaplain, the fleeting emotion felt in the service of ordination, the dullness and idleness of the young curate, who is seen at every dinner party and sometimes in the ballroom and at the race course. After a year this shallow youth goes to an elegant rectory. "He has exchanged the easy indifference of the idle curate for the self-importance and the authority of office of the idle rector." He now develops an interest in church architecture, in apostolic succession, and in abusing the Dissenters. Tayler regrets that many qualified men are obliged to live out their lives as impoverished curates while others quite unfit pass promptly to some important charge.

A mountain of similar information could be compiled. On the other hand, there were faithful and effective pastors of the kind described by Chaucer and Goldsmith, men not of leadership or of notable gifts, indeed, but of exemplary devotion to the duties of their office. They were undoubtedly exceptional, and most of them were under the influence of the Evangelical movement. So far as the Church of England was concerned, the Evangelicals were an embarrassing and embarrassed minority. They were not ecclesiastically minded, but were content to preach the gospel of conversion, to reform their own parishes, to promote missions to the distant heathen in his blindness, and to labor for the liberation of Negroes from slavery. Scarcely at all did they see as their problem the Erastian secularization of the Church of England. Their high seriousness was, of course, a constant testimony against the comfortable triflers who prospered on the incomes of the Church. They wrote a good many second-rate books, thereby exposing to the contempt of the learned their lack of intellectual and academic distinction.

It is often suggested that the Tractarians were transformed Evangelicals, and some of their number had indeed passed through a stage of Evangelicalism. But this is not true of Froude, Keble, or Pusey, to all of whom the Oxford doctrines were but new emphases and turns of interpretation upon basic and inherited convictions. In fact, the debt of the movement to Evangelicalism was largely that of countersuggestion. Intellectually the Oriel scholars were of the Brahmin caste and the Tractarians shared with their more liberal teachers the common contempt of privileged learning for a class to whom high scholarship is denied. The Evangelicals fully accepted the Reformation, from which the Tractarians were repelled, and they fraternized with Dissenters whom the Tractarians placed completely beyond the pale. It is true that Newman himself as a youth was profoundly affected by writings of leading Evangelicals, but he had emerged from these influences before his public career began.

The Tractarians had their antecedents among High-churchmen of the seventeenth century and such later favorers of the " catholic " interpretation of Anglicanism as Alexander Knox (1757–1831) and John Jebb (1775–1833). These Anglicans in Ireland asserted, though incidentally and unsystematically, positions on the sacraments that were substantially those later affirmed by Pusey. Keble, however, in a letter of October, 1838, expressed his displeasure at " Mr. Knox's admiration of Wesley and Co." Knox enjoyed a fruitful acquaintance with Wesley, whose mission he warmly approved; but his interests were more churchly and doctrinal than those of the evangelical apostle. Jebb, who was bishop of Limerick, as early as 1814 saw the possibility that through a persecuted movement there would come " an attachment to the Church as a hierarchy, as distinct from the State, and as dignified only by its intrinsic excellence, by its venerable antiquity and by its apostolic constitution."

II

Meanwhile there was growing evidence of a mounting crisis. The long agitation, successful in 1829, for " Catholic Emancipation " — the extension of citizenship rights and freedom of worship to Roman Catholics — had repercussions affecting Anglicanism. In many it aroused dire fears of Roman aggressiveness and consequent danger to the Church. A related question was that of curtailment of the extensive and expensive organization of the Established Church of Ireland, which was out of all proportion to its effectiveness. As early as 1824, John Jebb made an eloquent plea for its maintenance, before the House of Lords; but the day of reckoning was to come. Some have supposed that the French situation also had an influence in creating a new concern for the Church in England. In 1816, Lamennais had startled religionists by his *Essai sur l'indifférence,* which assailed the Bourbon regime as having subjected the French Church to debilitating oppression, and poured scorn on the Church of England as the model of secularity. In *L'Avenir,* a periodical which he with others founded, Lamennais called to the clergy to return to a primitive devotion.

Jeremy Bentham, the philosopher of secular liberalism, who looked upon the Church as a usable instrument of the benevolent State, had a wide influence that extended to the politicians. The idea began to gain attention that church revenues might advantageously undergo a redistribution at the hands of the Government. The pressure of the national Government upon the Church had produced a harvest of clerical secularity, and now the secular mind attacked Church and clergy on the secular ground of its excessive cost to the nation. In 1820 appeared anonymously *The Black Book, or Corruption Unmasked.* It was the work of John Wade, a journalist, a disciple of Bentham, and a protagonist of the new class of industrial workers. In 1831, after fourteen thousand copies had been sold, he put out a new and extensively revised edition, *The Extraordinary Black Book.*

In this work of exposure and propaganda, Wade generalizes on the unsatisfactory character of the clergy, who are said to resemble those of the pre-Reformation age, and to have supported every wrong public cause. He piles up statistics, and names names, on the shocking prevalence of pluralism and nonresidence. He attacks the system of tithes as without legal justification, and with tithes he would abolish patronage, which encourages simony and nepotism — of which offenses he cites numerous instances. He holds that the

Church's property, like that of the Army, should be kept in the control of the Government. His most popular argument lies in the charge that the Church is inordinately and injuriously wealthy ("a monstrous overgrown Croesus"), costing the country vastly more per capita than established Churches on the Continent and in Scotland, while its revenues go mainly to idlers who leave shamefully underpaid the "laboring bees" who substitute for them.

This vigorous and well-armed attack is of historical interest not only as the most important manifesto of its kind but because of the attitude to the establishment which it was calculated to evoke. Wade professes a desire not to cripple the Church but to reform it. But churchmen feared that it would produce a specific project for snatching the property of the Church, covetousness gaining its ends in the angelic guise of reform. A vague apprehension of this was in the air. It is well seen in a striking discourse of the Scottish Evangelical, Thomas Chalmers, in London (1829), *On the Use and Abuse of Literary and Ecclesiastical Endowments,* which contained denunciation of the "calculators and economists" who threatened the Church of England with "a truly Gothic spoliation."

Various reform proposals were being presented. In January of the fateful year 1833, one appeared from the pen of Thomas Arnold. This may be thought of as an ineffective Broad Church project that might have been the substitute for Tractarianism. Its appeal is to reason and good will, not to doctrine and tradition. Arnold would not confiscate the Church's wealth but devise ways of using it in the religious interests of the English people. By a revision of the Articles and liturgy he hoped to attract Nonconformists. He would have a bishop in every large town, and set up active diocesan assemblies. The ministry would be so distributed as "to provide in every parish the constant residence of one individual who has no other business than to do good of every kind to any person."

Numerous similar proposals then made for a new approach to Nonconformists are perhaps motivated by the fear that the latter would make common cause with the secular party of would-be reformers by confiscation. But a group of Oriel College scholars were about to launch a highly surprising series of tracts through which they would seize the initiative from Broad Church liberalism and assert High-Church doctrines with startling absolutism and uncompromising insistence.

III

Historians have brought to notice a dozen men whose views, expressed before 1833, show a strong resemblance to those of the Tractarians. This is really a testimony to the continuity of conceptions of the Church and the sacraments that were not uncommon in the seventeenth century but had rarely found expression amid the rationalism and Evangelicalism of the eighteenth. Whatever names may be associated with the background of the Oxford Movement, no one before John Keble can in any respect be looked upon as its founder.

Keble was an academic prodigy and a gentle, unassuming, cheerful, and brotherly soul, beloved by those who knew him, and exerting a quiet influence upon them. He was the son of a Gloucestershire vicar, won a double first class in Oxford, and at nineteen was elected a fellow of Oriel College (1811). This was eleven years before Newman gained that honor at the age of twenty-one. Richard Whately was at first Keble's most distinguished colleague, a brilliant liberal and dialectical defender of heretics, who later became archbishop of Dublin. Almost his equal, and a more circumspect thinker, was Thomas Arnold, who became master of Rugby in 1827. It may have been in part from a distaste for Whately's robust and confident assertion of unorthodox views that Keble chose to spend long periods in Devonshire villages where he could dance with, or preach to, the people with equal acceptance. Keble never was either a ponderous scholar or an austere saint. In 1827 appeared his celebrated book of poems, *The Christian Year*. It was something that the festivals of the Christian year should receive attention at all, but more significant that they were celebrated in memorable verse that soon had a wide circulation. The book set a new orientation of Christianity, honoring as it did old and half-forgotten traditions of the Church, not in the manner, but in the true spirit, of seventeenth century Anglican devotional poetry.

One who peruses the extensive published sermons of Keble will find little of a strongly controversial sort. But his assize sermon of July 14, 1833, on " National Apostasy," was a fighting discourse. The text was I Sam. 12:23, where Samuel says reproachfully to the people who have insisted on having a king, " God forbid that I should sin against the Lord in ceasing to pray for you: but I will teach you the good and the right way." Keble saw a godless and alarming trend in public policy. Wellington's ministry had been succeeded by that of Lord Gray. The Reform Bill of 1832 suppressed the " rotten boroughs " and enfranchised many industrial workers. It was followed by the election of a predominantly Whig parliament. The new secretary for Ireland devised the Church Temporalities Act, and this had the substantial approval of Whately, who had recently (1831) been made archbishop of Dublin. The act took no property from the Church of Ireland, while by the reduction of the number of dioceses it set free large sums for church construction and repair and to augment the stipends of ill-paid priests. But it was opposed by the Irish bishops because it suppressed the feeble dioceses and incorporated them in neighboring ones. To Keble, this was a wicked intrusion by a profane government in the affairs of the Church, and dramatic evidence of widespread apostasy. That the Tractarian Movement took its rise from this utterance is the statement of Newman, and it offers a convenient beginning date.

But the recoil against secular liberalism and Erastianism was already finding spokesmen. Newman had been preaching in a similar vein in St. Mary's, Oxford, and Hugh James Rose, vicar of Hadleigh, a Cambridge man, was editing a new journal, *The British Magazine,* to which Newman and Keble were contributors.

IV

Another personality of great force among the Tractarians was Richard Hurrell Froude. The son of an archdeacon, whom another son described as a High-churchman of the old school, Froude since 1821 had been a pupil of Keble, and had gained an influence over his tutor. Newman in his *Apologia* has well described Froude's personality and relation to the movement.

"I knew him first in 1826, and was in the closest and most affectionate friendship with him from about 1829 until his death in 1836. He was a man of the highest gifts."

Having referred to his "gentleness," "playfulness," "free elastic force and graceful versatility," Newman calls him

"a man of the highest genius, brimful and overflowing with ideas and views, in him original, which were too many and strong even for his bodily strength. . . . He professed openly his admiration of the Church of Rome and his hatred of the Reformers."

Tradition, as against the sole authority of Scripture, devotion to the Virgin Mary, and interest in saints and miracles were prominent in his conversation. "He was," says Newman, "powerfully drawn to the Medieval Church, but not to the Primitive. . . . He taught me to look with admiration towards the Church of Rome, and in the same degree to dislike the Reformation." Ebullient and sure of his opinions, he liked to pronounce judgments in unmeasured language, yet he was genuinely self-critical and devout. His repeated reading after 1826 of a diary kept by his mother, who had died in 1821, led him to realize that his early inconsiderateness had been a great trial to her, and to seek to tame his naturally assertive disposition. The record of his mother's concern and prayers for him moved him deeply. In his own journal he refers frequently to this:

"I did not recollect that I had been so unfeeling to her during her last year. . . . Everything I see in it [the diary] sends me back to her in my childhood: it gets such hold of me that I can hardly think of anything else."

His papers show too his penitence for a failure to appreciate the place of his father "as a type of the Almighty upon earth." Belated regret for unfilial conduct was thus a factor in the development of his religious personality. His exaggerated self-criticism reminds us, indeed, of typical Puritan diaries of the seventeenth century.

A disturbing fascination was exercised by this young scholar, with his blazing anger at Reformers and Evangelicals and his tender devotion to the miracle-working saints of the Middle Ages. John Henry Newman was two years Froude's senior, but it was Froude who impelled him on the course he was to follow. Newman came to Oxford a sixteen-year-old Protestant. His father, a London banker (whose bank had recently failed), and an admirer of Franklin and Jefferson, once said, " I do not pretend to be a religious man." But his mother was the devout descendant of a Huguenot family. John Henry's two brothers in different degrees showed the influence of their father, while he felt more that of his mother. On reading *The Arabian Nights,* he wondered, like many another boy, whether all life might be only a dream. He read books of the Evangelicals, of William Romaine and Thomas Scott and John Newton. Newton persuaded him that the pope was Antichrist, and Scott more profoundly stirred his spirit with phrases such as " holiness rather than peace " or " growth the only evidence of life." Newman in 1864 called Scott " the writer . . . to whom (humanly speaking) I almost owe my soul." Under these influences in 1816, he was conscious of an experience of conversion, and of the adoption of " a definite creed," which was Calvinistic. Yet the experience was accompanied by the un-Protestant decision that in accordance with God's will he would " lead a single life."

At Trinity College, Oxford, Newman was an austere and studious youth. In 1822 he became a fellow of Oriel. For five years thereafter he was a member of Whately's circle and his Evangelicalism was tempered by Liberalism. There were periods of deep religious anxiety, as shown by his correspondence with his mother. He was not to be satisfied with the liberalism of Whately, but shrank from its implications, and listened with fascination to the boldly expressed contrary opinions of Hurrell Froude. Froude prided himself on the fact that he brought Keble and Newman to mutual recognition and co-operation. At the same time Keble's *The Christian Year* (1827) impressed Newman with new thoughts of the Church's customs and traditions. An illness deepened his concern, and led to his study of the Church Fathers (1828). He was strongly drawn to the mystical and allegorical doctrines of the Alexandrians, and de-lighted in speculations on the angels. He had turned quite away from the Evangelicals of his own generation on the ground that "they played into the hands of the Liberals." If his soul was brought to life by the testimony of Scott and the Evangelicals, it now found its nourishment in other fields.

Newman's journey with Froude to Italy, 1832–1833, accentuated these impressions and rendered them vital. It was a time of liberal revolutions in Europe, and of the English Reform Bill and the Irish Temporalities Act, and Newman's heart was sick. "It was the suc-cess of the Liberal cause," he wrote, "that fretted me inwardly." This was the "encircling gloom" amid which he prayed for "kindly light" to lead him on into courageous service toward the restora-tion of the Catholic life of the Church of England. He reached England five days before Keble's famous sermon, Froude having preceded him.

V

After some correspondence with Keble and Newman, Froude and two others interested met with Rose in his parsonage at Hadleigh, Suffolk (July 25-29, 1833). Froude here showed complete dissatis-faction with the course favored by the others, of working for the rights of the Church through ecclesiastical channels. However, an address from the clergy to the archbishop of Canterbury was circu-lated, which received a surprising number of signatures. But Froude had earlier, in Trinity Gardens, Oxford, laid his hand on the shoul-der of his friend Isaac Williams (a learned convert of Keble from an irreligious life) and exclaimed, "Isaac, we must make a row in the world." In this spirit, Newman, without waiting for the ap-proval of the Hadleigh group or anyone else, began the series of daring manifestos entitled *Tracts for the Times,* September 9, 1833. The series was to end with the long and startling Tract 90, January 25, 1841. Of the ninety, twenty-nine were written by Newman, in-cluding the first and the last.

Midway in the production of the Tracts the movement was invigorated by the accession to its ranks of an eminent scholar. Edward Bouverie Pusey (1800–1882), fellow of Oriel and Regius Professor of Hebrew, had a High-Church Tory background and a German training. One of the early Tracts (on fasting, December 21, 1833) was by him, but he did not attach himself to the group until 1835, when he brought to Newman a learned tract, indeed a treatise on Baptism. In the following year he projected and began his *Library of the Fathers* in English, wishing to encourage the Tractarians by showing "that the Fathers are behind them." Newman welcomed the distinguished recruit, all the more eagerly because he was growing weary with the labor of the Tracts, but largely because of Pusey's reputation and scholarship: "He at once gave to us a position and a name." In some of the Tracts, Newman and other writers had made considerable use of Patristic extracts. The requirements of controversy were here, as often elsewhere in the history of the Church, the stimulus of a new historical scholarship. A new attention to the Fathers, with a rising sense of their authority, is one of the early fruits of the movement.

Along with the Fathers came the seventeenth century High-Church divines. Froude, who had no interest in Patristic studies and cultivated a contemptuous avoidance of the Reformers, pronounced encomiums upon the seventeenth century exponents of high doctrines of the Church. Newman, in his important Tract 38, *Via media,* remarks, "In the seventeenth century the theology of the divines of the English Church was substantially the same as ours." In proof that the trend of the Tracts is not "popish" he adds that this theology then "experienced the full hostility of the papacy." In his *Apologia* he observes that the aim of the group was "a new Reformation — a return not to the sixteenth century but to the seventeenth." In addition to the *Library of the Fathers* there soon appeared (1841) a *Library of Anglo-Catholic Theology,* which contained the works of selected seventeenth century churchmen. Keble had led the way to this by his still valuable edition of Hooker's works (1836). Such seventeenth century scholars as Launcelot Andrews, William Laud, John Cosin, Herbert Thorndike, Jeremy Taylor, and George Bull offered genuine support for many of the Tractarian positions.

VI

The Tracts of 1833 were collected and published in a volume in 1834 with a preface in which it was stated that their object was the revival of doctrines held by the great divines of the Church of England but recently " obsolete with the majority of her members." These include apostolic succession, and the doctrine that " the sacraments, not preaching, are the sources of divine grace." Methodism and popery are foster mothers of the Church's abandoned children. The revival of these doctrines will establish a union of true Christians against " the extension of popery." This alarm against " popery " is much stressed in the early Tracts; perhaps not the less because Newman was aware that an opposite intention might be ascribed to his teaching. " I expect to be called a papist when my opinions are known," he wrote, November 22, 1833. Several of the Tracts stress the importance of the doctrine of the divine authority of the Church as a means of maintaining the Church of England against the papacy. God, he observes, in Tract 20,

" has wonderfully preserved our Church as a true branch of the Church Universal, yet withal preserved it free from doctrinal error. It is Catholic and apostolic, yet not papistical."

To the members of other communions the Tractarians gravely award an inferior citizenship in the Kingdom of Heaven, or else frankly exclude them therefrom. Newman declines in any " false charity " to exempt the Scottish Presbyterians from the condemnation of the Samaritans implied in the words of Jesus, " Ye worship ye know not what: we know what we worship." There is a graduated scale of divine favor, the Protestant sects " lie between us and heathenism," and the grades descend through Judaism, Islam, Hinduism, the North American Indians (theists), to polytheism. What is called an orthodox sect has a portion of that divine favor which is withheld from heresy (Tract 47).

The superiority of Anglicanism was made to rest largely upon the affirmation of the apostolical succession of its bishops. In two Tracts (29, 30) on Christian liberty by a layman (John W. Bowden)

there runs a dialogue between a rector and a parishioner who has been attracted by the earnest preaching of a Dissenting minister. The rector leads the erring one to ask, " Who are these successors of the apostles in our country? " and receives the simple answer, " The bishops of the Church of England are they " — and Dissenters have no such claim. Later it is explained that, while papists are called Catholics, " it is we that are the true Catholics."

The Reformation era had produced the main official statements of Anglicanism. The Tractarians felt obliged to explain these documents and not to repudiate them. Newman's argument (38) is that the Thirty-nine Articles are not a body of divinity but a protest against certain errors; hence their omission of doctrines now stressed that belong to " the *whole* gospel." It has been frivolously stated " that we have Calvinistic articles and a papist liturgy." The real distinction is that the liturgy is from the apostles and the Articles are polemical. Other points are now to be stressed: " Times are changed. We are in danger of unbelief more than of superstition." Something was added to this pattern of thought in the elaborate argument of Tract 90, " Remarks on Certain Passages in the Thirty-nine Articles," with which the series came to a dramatic close.

Here not only the Prayer Book but the Articles themselves are treated as, in the slightly modified language of Ralph Chillingworth, " patient though not ambitious of a Catholic interpretation." Newman had already " begun to wish for union " with Rome, and to urge his friends to pray for this. His recently converted associate William George Ward, a man whose qualities resembled those of the now deceased Froude, seems to have urged him to write this essay, and Keble approved it before it went to the printer. But, to the author's astonishment, it shocked the Anglican public far more violently than any previous Tract.

Tract 90 is, indeed, a surprising piece. Newman is not interested in what the framers of the Articles wanted them to affirm, but in making them affirm, or rather permit, doctrines acceptable to Roman Catholics. A good example is the treatment of Article xxii, which condemns as " repugnant to the Word of God " the Romish doctrine of purgatory, worship of images, and adoration of saints. It is said that the doctrine of purgatory, images, etc., that is condemned is not the primitive doctrine of these, nor the Catholic doctrine, nor that of the Council of Trent, but something else called *doctrina Romanensium,* which is rather vaguely treated by references to medieval tales. Although Newman argues that in interpreting the Articles " we have no duties toward their framers," he points out that they were framed before the decisions of the Council of Trent and could not have been designed to contradict these. He also argues that the Articles were " principally drawn " (!) from the writings of Melanchthon, who was charged with " popery "; that they were so framed as to " leave open large questions" and " to comprehend those who did not go so far in Protestantism " as their compilers.

Why this new attempt to find accord with Rome? His Anglicanism had formerly been confidently superior to Romanism. But here is Anglicanism tested by, and brought into a highly uncomfortable accord with, Roman beliefs. Since the autumn of 1839, Newman was, as he put it, "a man who has seen a ghost." The specter was presented by an article on " The Anglican Claim," by Nicholas Patrick (later Cardinal) Wiseman in *The Dublin Review.* To this learned Irishman born in Seville, the " Anglican claim " was as groundless as that of the Donatists of old. The article contained an apt quotation from Saint Augustine in condemnation of the Donatists, a phrase of which was singled out by a friend of Newman and forced upon his consideration: "*Securus judicat orbis terrarum* " — the whole world is a safe judge. Newman did not have the protection of T. A. Lacey's able treatment of the Augustine passage (*Catholicity,* 1914, Appendix B) with his suggestion for turning the argument against Wiseman. Dr. Lacey rightly points to the incidents of April, 1833, reported in Froude's papers (*Remains* I, 306) which Keble had published. Newman and Froude when in Rome consulted Dr. Wiseman and asked of him the terms of admission to the Roman communion. The reply, as stated by Froude, required at the outset unqualified acceptance of " the atrocious Council of Trent." Froude was so offended that at the time he " wished for the total overthrow of their system."

In the *Review* article Wiseman was giving the same answer in

another form. The Roman Church is *orbis terrarum:* it speaks with
the voice of the true Church in all the world. The Church of England is a detached fragment, severed from the realm of grace. This
is Newman's ghost. " The *via media,*" he says, " was absolutely pul-
verized." The ghost quite softened Newman's tone toward Rome.
His adherents felt this change in him, and the more impetuous of
them hastened to Rome before him. This embarrassed and grieved
him. He was weary, hypersensitive, and discouraged. He had fought
a hard battle, laboring over the Tracts and keeping up a series of
sermons in St. Mary's Church that some felt to be even more influential than the Tracts themselves. As a preacher he had shown an almost mesmeric power of persuasion. He had acquired a large student
following, and from Ward, who had been converted to Tractarianism
by his preaching, the undergraduates took up the habit of reciting
with fervor a new creed — " *Credo in Newmanum.*" But now the
leader could not lead, or restrain, his admirers. His old ecclesiastical
convictions were being dissolved. At the same time Liberalism was
aggressive and terrifying. Something must be tried. Tract 90 was a
venture in high strategy. Could Anglicanism be revived and unified
on the basis of a recognition of Rome as the true Church? Newman
had observed that he was as one who proves a cannon, knowing that
it may explode disastrously.

The cannon exploded. Anglicanism had strength enough to utter
a thunderous, " No." The argument of the Tract was not only
unconvincing, but shocking and exasperating. Even today its interpretations leave the reader bewildered. It is not surprising that many
thought it dishonest. A similar treatment of the Ten Commandments would utterly undermine morality.

The Heads of Houses who governed the university condemned
the Tract as having " evaded rather than explained " the Articles.
The bishop of Oxford induced Newman to discontinue the Tracts.
Individual disciples preceded him to Rome: we need not here follow
the process by which he became prepared to follow them. He had
already reached the end of the road as an exponent of Anglicanism,
and now he was repudiated by the Church. Not collectively, but in
personal utterances, most of the bishops unequivocally condemned

the Tract and its author. Wounded and defeated, Newman allowed every fresh experience to carry him on toward the scene of October 9, 1845, when Father Dominic of the Passionist Order, the son of an Italian peasant, received the great convert into what the latter now called " the One Fold of the Redeemer."

VII

The Oxford Movement had enlisted a man of more steadfast churchmanship than Newman and of greater boldness and originality than Keble. The burden of leadership now fell upon Edward Bouverie Pusey. Pusey was unshaken in his Anglicanism, because, unlike Newman, while advocating apostolic succession in the episcopate, he had never counted upon the living English bishops to support the movement. Instead, he fundamentally " trusted the Church of England." He had never felt the inclination to go to Rome for refuge from the untoward conditions in the Church of his fathers. He was now to become the central figure in the movement, and to fix its impress upon the Church. Although it is an Oxford scholar who is now to guide the course of the movement, Oxford is no longed to have the unique importance in it that was so marked in the beginning. The whole Church is now concerned with it, and it calls forth a response also in other churches of Britain, the British dominions, America, and Continental Europe. From the time of Newman's departure from Oxford (1843) we may conveniently speak, not of the Oxford Movement, but of the Anglo-Catholic Revival.

Pusey had been among the first Englishmen to come into contact with nineteenth century German theological scholarship. He returned from Germany in 1827 equipped by Old Testament studies. He moderately defended his German teachers against the warnings of Hugh James Rose, but subsequently found himself largely in accord with Rose and in full revolt against the rationalism and theological indifference of the Germans. A laborious worker, Pusey came slowly before the public, and was not well known personally even to those who admired his learning and devout conduct. As a scholar he outclassed the other Tractarians. The death of his wife (who had worn herself out in charities and as his secretary) in 1839 caused him to retire into a life of seclusion and great austerity. He regarded her death as a punishment upon him for his sins. He held himself inferior to all whom he met, wore haircloth, ate unappetizing food, and when he lay down in bed, made a point of remembering that he was unworthy to lie anywhere but in hell. Yet he was gentle and tender toward his three (surviving) children and beloved by them. Through his writings Dr. Pusey became the highly respected exponent of doctrines and practices by which Anglicanism was being gradually transformed into something widely different from what it had been. Pusey was not, needless to say, the sole agent in this transformation, but his part in it was an indispensable one. He was, as Newman said, " a man of large designs."

One of his designs was the restoration of ascetic community life. The idea had been awakened in other minds. Nicholas Ferrar in the seventeenth century and William Law in the eighteenth had dreamed of such a revival, and in some degree engaged in the practice of group asceticism. During the French Revolution refugee French Roman Catholic nuns and monks of different orders formed communities in England, and were admired for their devotion and charity. Robert Southey the poet wrote in 1829, on returning from the Continent where he had observed ascetic women engaged in services to the people: " Thirty years hence . . . England may have its Beguines and its Sisters of Charity. It is grievously in need of them." Pusey's daughter Lucy (d. 1844) early expressed an intention of entering a sisterhood. In 1839, Pusey discussed the matter with Newman, who agreed that the Church of England should have Sisters of Charity; and he later freely expressed this view in ways that called forth numerous inquiries from devout ladies. To one of these, Marian Rebecca Hughes, he administered a vow of chastity in 1841. When Southey died in 1843, Lord John Manners proposed as a memorial to him the establishment of a Sisterhood of Mercy. Authorization was secured from the bishop of London. Pusey himself made a handsome gift of money for a building near Regent's Park. A good many besides Pusey were now eager to see the upgrowth of ascetic communities, and monastic ideals were already being advocated by Isaac Taylor, John Mason Neale, William Ewart Gladstone, and other prominent sympathizers with Tractarianism. Yet none took the initiative in the matter as Pusey did. He collected foreign Roman Catholic books on the subject, visited houses of nuns in Ireland, and through friends procured information on orders in France. Miss Hughes herself visited Normandy for this purpose.

In promoting sisterhoods, Pusey had the co-operation of Lydia Sellon, a naval captain's daughter and a woman of great energy and Catholic devotion, who had paid a visit to Pusey's London foundation in 1847. Miss Sellon with courage and enterprise engaged in the reclamation and education of neglected children (" little savages ") and gathered about herself a sisterhood at Devonport and Plymouth — " the Church of England Sisterhood of Mercy " (1848). Pusey kept in close touch with both the communities, and heard the confessions of the Sisters, who called him " Father." Charges regarding Catholic ceremonies were made against Miss Sellon and Dr. Pusey, but were dismissed on investigation by the bishop of Exeter as referring to acts not out of accord with the Prayer Book. But calumnious rumors persisted, and it was necessary to deny in the *Times* that Pusey and the Lady Superior had been married. The Sisters recovered the good will of the people by their heroic service during a cholera epidemic. Troubles, however, continued to disturb the Sisterhood. Very " high " elements of ceremonial were introduced, and the household was not always in accord. One nun so starved herself in Lent, 1851, that she died, having first received extreme unction from a Scottish bishop. There were secessions to Rome, and one girl was actually abducted for her salvation by one of the seceders; she soon escaped. For many years Miss Sellon lived in a storm of rumored and published accusations. Expansion in numbers led to elaboration of the rules, and a damaging attack was made by Margaret Goodman, who withdrew from the house on account of alleged harsh austerity, cruelty, and hypocrisy (1861). Miss Sellon's biographer, T. J. Williams, implies the falsity of these charges, but one who reads Miss Goodman's two books will wish that he had dealt more substantially with their contents.

Other Sisterhoods arose without Pusey's personal co-operation. Thomas Carter at Clewer established an institute for the recovery of prostitutes, and John Mason Neale formed St. Margaret's Sisterhood (1856) at East Grinstead, a nursing society serving in the homes of the people. St. Margaret's opened branches and schools in many places and became an important agency in religiously motivated social service. The Roman Catholic Sisters of Charity founded by St. Vincent de Paul, and the Lutheran deaconess order founded by Theodor Fliedner, were among the models that had influence in its development. These and various later sisterhoods and houses of nuns in Anglicanism offered new opportunities of religious discipline and service for many women who would otherwise have led ineffective and frustrated lives.

Orders of men were advocated and introduced rather later. Clerical celibacy was favored by the Tractarians, and at a late stage before his conversion, Newman gathered a small celibate community at Littlemore. Under Pusey's influence John Leycester Syne (" Father Ignatius ") established a house of men that was an Anglican modification of the Benedictine Order: later a nunnery was added. Another Benedictine organization, having settled at Calday Island, seceded in a body to the Roman obedience (1913). The Society of St. John the Evangelist, founded at Cowley (hence " Cowley Fathers ") by Richard Meux Benson in 1866, designedly held in balance the contemplative and active phases of devotion; it has been concerned in foreign missions. The Community of the Resurrection, founded by Charles Gore in 1887, has been likened to the French Oratory, and like the latter has had intellectual distinction. Gore, Henry Scott Holland, and others were at this period to impart to Anglo-Catholicism a new spirit of social concern which has been a mark of the movement ever since.

VIII

Pusey was also prominent in the revival, amid controversy, of Roman Catholic features of worship and interpretations of the sacraments. His sermon, *The Holy Eucharist a Comfort to the Peni-*

tent, 1843, advocating the corporeal presence, was published with an array of supporting quotations from Anglican divines. In 1853 he preached eloquently on *The Presence of Christ in the Holy Eucharist.* His doctrine of the bodily presence, as he was careful to point out repeatedly, was presented with a view to "the comfort of the penitent."

The element of penitence in the Oxford Movement can be traced in various personal histories, in none more clearly than in Pusey's own. Another of his great sermons, *Entire Absolution of the Penitent,* 1846, presents in urgent terms a Churchly doctrine of oft-repeated penitence and absolution. "Penitent thyself," says Pusey here, "thou shalt learn to speak to the hearts of penitents." Pusey, Keble, and others of the new school in their spiritual consultations made use of secret confession, which at that time was widely regarded as the mark of Romanism; and they had a wide following among the clergy. An impressive petition in favor of "sacramental penance" was presented to the Convocation of Canterbury (1873). The public was so aroused that a "Declaration of Confession and Absolution" was published in the *Times* (December 6, 1873), largely the work of Pusey. In this notable declaration the practice of confession is supported from the Prayer Book and Homilies. It is argued that we may not infer from the provision for confession in the office of Visitation of the Sick that Anglicans are "bound to defer to a deathbed what they know to be good for their souls." The strife continued, and with it the growth of confession and absolution. Pusey made selective use of Roman Catholic interpretations of the confessional, and in 1877 he published a translation of the Abbé Jean Joseph Gaume's *Manual for Confessors,* a compilation from Roman Catholic authorities. The edition was pruned of Mariolatry and other objectionable elements of piety, and was accompanied by a long preface supporting the confessional by citation of Anglican documents and of divines from Cranmer to Keble.

Pusey and his associates did not shrink from battle and their lives were lived in the stress of controversy. But there was emerging an increasing concern for reunion, and many of those who did not follow Newman and Ward to the Roman fold still sought a basis of agreement with the papacy. Although Newman had abandoned the *via media* conception of Anglicanism when he wrote Tract 90, Pusey retained the *via media* while always defending Tract 90 in substance. But, in distinction from Newman, Pusey always favored mutual accord and ultimate reunion with the Greek Church. William Palmer, an early Tractarian, gave great attention to this matter, awakening a growing acquaintance particularly with the Russian Church by his historical studies.

Cardinal Wiseman encouraged Anglo-Catholics to look hopefully for a response from Rome, and favored the formation in 1857 of the Association for the Promotion of the Unity of Christendom; but the published organ of the Association proved a battleground, and Roman Catholics were forbidden to hold membership in the organization (1864). The former Anglican Cardinal Henry Edward Manning took occasion soon afterward to speak of the Church of England as " the Mother of all the aberrations " of the time. Dr. Pusey's reply to this grew into the first *Eirenicon* which took the form of a letter to Keble (1865). As the full title indicates, it presents the Church of England as " a portion of Christ's only Catholic Church and a means of restoring visible unity." A second and a third *Eirenicon* followed (1869–1870), each addressed to Newman, who had attacked the first unmercifully. Pusey had suggested that not only the Articles but the decisions of Trent required "interpretation," and had not failed to assail elements in the Roman Catholic cultus. The Vatican Council's declaration of papal infallibility, 1870, quite discouraged Pusey from further approaches to Rome. Meanwhile John Mason Neale had been instrumental in founding the Eastern Church Association (1863). This was the beginning of a fresh interest in Eastern Orthodoxy, which has grown in Anglicanism with the lapse of time.

IX

The Tractarian Movement and its outcome in Anglo-Catholicism gave expression to realities of religious experience and tradition that the children of the Reformation had repudiated or ceased to prize. Like the Evangelicals before them, the Tractarians assailed the spirit of secularity with zeal and courage. The leaders were saintly men, following their consciences at any cost. They were " saintly " too in the ascetic sense, and their devoutness strengthened their cause. They set themselves to win converts, not benefices, and often exhibited a beautiful unworldliness. Even if they gave utterance to prejudiced judgments, they endured prejudice and misunderstanding from others without becoming soured. The flippant anathemas of Froude were not characteristic of the constructive leaders. They brought to their Church and other Churches a new awareness of the value of disciplined devotion, a new consciousness of the importance of the sacramental, and an emphasis (especially in *Lux Mundi,* 1889, an Anglo-Catholic symposium to combat impressions made by science and criticism) upon the doctrine of the incarnation. Their high doctrine of the Church and the ministry, though couched in terms unacceptable to a majority of thoughtful Christians, had a beneficial impact upon Christianity in general, creating everywhere a revival of a feeling for the Holy Catholic Church as in each denomination it was affirmed. A bishop who did not favor their ecclesiastical ideals confessed: " They have been the chief instruments in reviving the study of sound theology . . . they have raised the standard of the ministerial character." This result appeared in all parts of the Anglican communion, and was carried far beyond its limits.

The weaknesses of Anglo-Catholicism are, however, patent. It began in fear of secularism and was long haunted by fear. It shrank in dread from Biblical criticism and evolutionary science as Newman (who never read a line of Kant), fearing for his soul, had turned his back upon " liberalism." They unduly minimized the service of reason to religion. The use they made of history was not such as to commit the mind to its broad facts, but to search for proof texts that could be assembled out of context in imposing catenae. The Tractarians established in a great part of Anglicanism a habit of contempt toward the Reformation and a neglect of its writers. Froude thought Cranmer could be credited with one thing only: " he burnt well." To burn well was not enough, and when the Martyrs' Monument was set up in Oxford (1841), the Tractarians refused to contribute or approve. The coldness of Pusey's references to the Reformation is well illustrated in a sermon of 1837, on the anniversary of the Gunpowder Plot, which contains a long passage on the Massacre of St. Bartholomew. He blames the papacy for persecution, marvels at the incautious behavior of the " foreign Protestants," and, avoiding any expression of sympathy for the sufferers, gives thanks to God that the Church of England escaped such calamities. Keble praises Hooker in the degree in which Hooker differs from Cranmer and approaches Laud. Providence, he thought, had overruled the Reformation, leaving the way open for a retreat from it to " antiquity." Anglo-Catholicism unquestionably regained values that the Reformation neglected, but not less certainly its rejection of the positive contributions of the Reformation has entailed serious religious limitation and loss.

Those whose souls flourish in the simplicities of Protestant worship, and to whom elaborate ceremonial is a detriment to devotion, are alienated from Anglo-Catholicism by its entanglement in " ritualism." It should be remembered in the first place that the early Anglo-Catholics were distinctly opposed to the new attention to ceremonial " externals." Pusey wore very plain garb at the altar, and thought that rich vestments would minister to vanity. While he pointed out the force of some forgotten rubrics of the Prayer Book, he did not favor enforcing the ornaments rubric, which required the vestments of " the second year of Edward VI." It is pointed out by S. L. Ollard that " the first dawn of the ceremonial revival preceded the Oxford Movement by ten years." There is no reason why it might not have prospered without the Tractarians. Yet the Ritualists clung to the Tractarians, and in the end gained a virtually complete victory for what certain bishops of the time called " frippery " and " mummery." It was, however, a wholesome check upon the " gingerbread " school, that J. M. Neale, having founded the Camden Society when an undergraduate at Cambridge (1839) for ecclesiological studies, applied sound knowledge to the added ceremonial of vestments, gestures, and hymnody. Many bishops attempted to suppress these highly controversial changes, but without legal justification, and ineffectively. By the 1870's Anglo-Catholics were commonly spoken of as " Ritualists." Even when the Privy Council gave an adverse judgment on certain points of ceremonial (1871), and when legislation was enacted to make these an offense, many priests went willingly to prison rather than submit. The struggle ended with the Convocation effectively resisting state compulsion, so that on the issue of ceremonial a defeat was administered to the Erastian System against which the early Tractarians had protested on other grounds. This result was in part made possible by the fact that the Church had regained its corporate voice. The restoration of Convocation, which had been silenced since 1718, took effect in 1861, largely as a result of the new spirit created by the Oxford Movement.

Thus the autonomy of the Church had in large degree become a reality. In Scotland this result was obtained at the cost of the Great Disruption of 1843 and a long period of separation; but by 1921 the principle of Church autonomy was fully established by the Scottish Churches Act. The Church of England is still not so happily related to the State, yet it is far from being an oppressed Church. It is still somewhat disturbed within by the stresses of the Tractarian strife, but it has undeniably advanced far in spirituality and vision since the movement began; and in this advance virtually all parts of the Christian Church in some way share. Keble's view that the Reformation was providentially overruled for good may be applied to the exaggerated emphases in Anglo-Catholicism itself, while from its excellences it has been a quickening force in modern Christianity.

Chapter
5

THE ECUMENICAL MOVEMENT IN HISTORICAL PERSPECTIVE

I

W hat gracious heart is not cut asunder with grief for those sore and fearful evils that there are in, and come from, our divisions, and is not even the second time cut asunder with careful thoughts in itself, what may be done to heal them? " So Richard Baxter begins his discourse on *The Cure of Church Divisions* (1670). If he were with us now, he would need only to modernize the form, and not to change the substance, of this rhetorical question. " That they all may be one " remains a prayer. Yet we may begin to see a new answer to the prayer in our time.

Two drives have constantly marked the Church's history, one toward expansion; the other toward integration. Expansion into new areas and peoples entails the peril of sectionalism and division. Against these the very nature of Christianity protests. The Church affirms and seeks to realize its unity. In anxiety to secure this it has sometimes resorted to high claims of legal authority and reliance upon compulsion by secular governments. This condition was characteristic of the medieval period as a whole. It called forth, however, reactions of heresy and schism, which could sometimes be crushed but never eradicated. Thus the means employed to assure unity were a psychological cause of disunity. The medieval Church reached a point in the growth of sectarian movements in which the exclusion and persecution of sectaries, as heretics and schismatics, began to suggest the very dismemberment of the body of the Church.

The Reformation protested against the compulsion of conscience, yet retained elements of this, justifying these on grounds of security against anarchy and of obedience to the Scripture. But Protestantism had no success in the compulsory restraint of variation and divisiveness. To declare, as Calvinism did, that "God alone is Lord of the conscience," and yet to persecute those whose consciences revolted from a prescribed doctrine or ceremony, did not make sense. As it violated logic it violated also human feeling. This is seen as early as 1575 in the plea of John Foxe the martyrologist to Queen Elizabeth on behalf of accused Anabaptists:

"I do not write thus from any bias to the indulgence of error, but to save the lives of men, being myself a man."

A more secular humanitarianism later arose, which helped to make compulsion in religion repugnant to the modern mind. Restraint on belief and persecution of heretics survive as a vestigial reminder of their former importance, and chiefly in areas where Protestantism is of inconsiderable strength. Nothing would more astonish a sixteenth century martyr who might revisit the world than to find that in our century persecution is far more antireligious than religious. Most Christians of today are fully convinced that Church unity is to be sought by other means than compulsion.

Yet the urge toward a comprehensive unity of the Christian Church never was stronger or more vigorously manifested than now. While the heart of the kindly Puritan would again be " cut asunder " on viewing the evils of division if he were with us now, he would find some compensating encouragement in the achievement of men of a spirit like his during the last hundred years. Thanks to their faith and labor, there has arisen a powerful unitive movement in Christianity that demands and creates the organizational framework of a world-wide spiritual fellowship in which unnumbered Christians share.

II

How this has come about is a long and complicated story that " many have taken in hand to set forth in order " (Luke 1:1), and that can be brought to notice here only in part and with great brevity. The whole history of the Church may be interpreted in terms of the effort to gain or maintain its integration and the corporate unity of its geographically extended body. Great rifts and secessions occurred in the early centuries, and the medieval Church brought forth a bewilderingly numerous brood of sects. From the beginning of the Reformation the problem of schism haunted Christian leaders more than ever. It was Luther's early hope to draw into communion with the Western Church both the Greek Orthodox and the Bohemian Hussites who had been severed from the papacy. He repeatedly appealed for a free general council that would institute measures of reform for all Christendom. As Protestantism began to form families of churches, zealous efforts were made to forestall disruption or attain unity. Martin Bucer, John à Lasco, John Calvin, and Theodore Beza were among those who in the sixteenth century spent much energy seeking to advance this cause. As Christ is Head of the Church, they believed, it is by its proper nature one in him. The children of Geneva were taught that the Holy Catholic Church is called catholic or universal because:

" as there is but one Head of all believers, so they must all be united in one body, that the Church diffused through the whole world may be one, and not more,"

and that through the communion of saints all the faithful participate in " whatever benefits God bestows upon the Church."

This was characteristic teaching. John Jewel, speaking for the Church of England in 1562, admirably expresses the common Reformation view:

" We believe that there is one Church of God, and that not confined, as it was heretofore, to the Jewish people, in one angle or kingdom, but that it is catholic and universal, and so diffused or spread over the face of the whole earth that there is no nation that can justly claim that it is excluded . . . that Christ is the only prince of this kingdom " (*Apology for the Anglican Church*, ii, 6).

Although the Reformers emphasized the spiritual and invisible aspect of the Church, they also taught that the Catholic Church of the Apostles' Creed is visible wherever the gospel is truly preached and the sacraments are rightly administered. They would all have approved in substance the Westminster Confession of Faith (1647) in its statements:

" The visible Church, which is also catholic or universal under the gospel (not confined to one nation, as before under the law), consists of all those throughout the world that profess the true religion, together with their children; and is the Kingdom of the Lord Jesus Christ, the house and family of God, out of which there is no ordinary possibility of salvation. . . . This catholic Church hath been sometimes more, sometimes less, visible. . . . There is no head of the church but the Lord Jesus Christ" (XXV, ii, iv, vi).

The emphasis on Christ's headship of the Church was set over against the papal headship. The unity sought was to be expressed not by obedience to a pope alleged to hold authority as successor of Peter, but through councils representing the Church in all its parts, guided by the Holy Spirit and free from papal control. This was in substance the doctrine of the Conciliarists of the fourteenth and the early fifteenth century. It had been formally declared in high terms at the Council of Constance in 1415, and roundly condemned in 1460 by Pope Pius II. From an early stage the Reformers varied the teaching of the Conciliarists by a specific exclusion of the pope. " A free general Christian council " was the oft-reiterated demand of Luther and of Calvin. In fact, a council for general pacification and reform was the pipe dream of the Reformation age. Emperors and kings favored settlement by a council, hoping to exert a determining influence upon it. The only actual religious council that could in some sense be called " general " was that of Trent; but it was not truly representative and it was not free.

Nevertheless, as countless documents show, the conciliar hope of a unified Church representatively governed was always a factor in the thoughts and plans of Protestant leaders. In a memorandum written by Calvin in December, 1560, during a ten-year interruption of the Council of Trent, and when a treaty between French and Imperial rulers had caused new talk of a general settlement, we read one of the numerous proposals of this sort. The Reformer states that "a free and universal council" is needed "to put an end to the existing divisions of Christianity." It must be free with respect to place of meeting, membership, and discussion, and bound only by Scripture. He recommends, for convenience and fairness to all, a location central to the peoples represented. The main points in doctrine, worship, and polity to be discussed and determined are set down. A national synod may enact reforms for the national area, but only a genuinely universal council, he affirms, can heal the miseries of Christendom. In the light of such appeals as this it is hardly surprising that Protestantism has generally adopted conciliar, or representative polities, or that the ecumenical movement should produce a World Council of Churches.

National differences, political disturbances, widespread wars, difficulties of travel, theological disputes, indifference, and bigotry were factors in the failure of these brave hopes. The seventeenth century saw schism upon schism. Countless zealous sects and autonomous movements appeared. While Baxter grieved, the great bishop of Meaux, Jacques Bénigne Bossuet, described in another mood "the variations of Protestantism" as proofs of its inherent perversity derived from the inconstancies of Luther and the "dizzy madness in his head." The Puritan revolt in England and the execution of King Charles I are evidence to him that Protestantism is the fruit of a spirit of disruption, destructive of social order and political security. This view is still reflected in the work of numerous historians, although it fails to account for the relative political security of Protestant countries and the sincere quest of religious unity by innumerable Protestant leaders. The coming disintegration and extinction of Protestantism is still a dogma within the eschatology of some of its adversaries. These prophets fail to observe that when it divides it is not in all cases disintegration that ensues, but sometimes fresh energy and growth, and that severed Protestant Churches are sometimes reunited in firmer bonds than before.

Nevertheless, Protestantism has been plagued by schism and sectarianism. It has lacked the firm restraint of unified authority and has ordinarily employed no means except persuasion of checking wayward or radical thought. It has encouraged freedom of opinion and discussion. The historic fact of the Reformation tends to create a psychological readiness for another reformation anywhere and at any time, and an unwillingness to quench any " new light " that may " break forth." If a denomination becomes anxiously protective of its beliefs and practices, it is the more apt to give birth to a minority group convinced of possessing fresh illumination. Thus we have reached a stage of fragmentation that neither Baxter nor Bossuet saw.

III

For a long time the splintering up of the Protestant communions was scarcely even retarded by the protests and activities of those who deplored and sought to reverse the trend. The efforts of these devoted apostles of unity in unfavorable times constitute a fascinating story with heroic episodes. The man whom Baxter most admired for his labors on behalf of Protestant unity was John Dury (1596–1680), a resourceful Scot who spent half a century in undiscouraged, if apparently unfruitful, activity in the cause of ecumenical unity during what he called a " contentious and dividing age." Letters and treatises poured from his pen; he traveled widely and conferred with countless men of distinction in church and public life. Some of those he consulted co-operated with him, some were indifferent, and some were hostile. He may be charged with impatience and ineptitude, and with a failure to realize fully the force of denominational habits and national feeling. In the light of later history, his projects appear utopian. Like others of his age, he looked to the rulers of States to aid his reforms. While he was deeply interested in education and pastoral theology and wrote ably on these topics, he did not succeed in getting the ideas that moved him conveyed to the lay mind. While he made his testimony in many fine utterances and in a life of devotion, he did not become the founder of a movement that would show cumulative force.

Still, leaders of the present-day ecumenical movement might in some sense call him their predecessor. His idea, as first set forth amply in his *Method of Procedure* (1632), involved a sequence of conferences. Difficulties within German Lutheranism and within the Reformed Churches would be ironed out in the first series of these meetings; then the negotiations would be taken up in joint conferences; and finally all evangelical Churches of Europe, including those of Britain, would send representatives to a General Assembly to frame a consensus for all the Churches. There is something here that is prophetic of twentieth century developments: the project is far more complex than the sixteenth century proposal for one deliberative and legislative general council.

Dury was for a time personally associated with Baxter (in a Church co-operation plan for Worcestershire) and Baxter published favorable accounts of Dury's activities abroad. But in *The True Catholic* (1660), one of Baxter's many writings in the cause of unity, he expressed feelings of depression over the misunderstanding and mischief that often arose in response to such well-meant efforts as Dury's, and the great difficulties placed in the way of their success:

" It is a pitifull case with the poor afflicted Church of Christ, that almost all her Members cry out against Division, and yet cause and increase it, while they speak against it. And that all cry up Unity, and yet very few do any thing that's very considerable to promote it; but multitudes are destroying Unity, while they commend it: And those few that would heal and close the wounds, are not able by the clearest reasons, and most importunate requests, to hold the hands of others from opposing it; and to get leave of the rest to do that work, which they will not do themselves while they extoll it. You would think this were rather the description of a Bedlam, than of a Christian! To set all on fire, and furiously to rail at all that would quench it, and at the same time to rail as much at incendiaries, and cry out for Concord, and against Division, and call other men all that's naught, for doing that which they do themselves, and will not be perswaded from? . . . Nay sinne gets advantage in point of Reputation, and Dividing is counted a work of Zeal, and Ministers themselves are the principal leaders of it; yea and Ministers of eminent parts and piety; and piety itself is pretended for this, which is the poison of piety: and pacification is become a suspected or derided work; and the Peacemakers are presently suspected of some heresie; and perhaps call'd Dividers for seeking Reconciliation. It made my heart ake with grief, the other day, to read over the Narrative of the endeavours of one man (M. John Dury) to heal the Protestant Churches themselves, and to think that so much ado should be necessary to make even the leaders of the Christian flocks to be willing, to cease so odious a sinne, and come out of so long and dolefull a misery; yea, and that all should do so little good, and get from men but a few good words, while they can sit still and suffer the flames to consume the deplorable remnant: Yea such havock hath division made, and cut the Church into so many pieces, that it is become one of the commonest Questions among us, which of these pieces it is that is the Church: One saith, *We are the Catholick Church;* and another saith, *No, but it is We!* and a third contendeth, that it is *onely they:* and thus men seem to be at a losse, and when they believe the *holy Catholick Church,* they know not what it is, which they say, they believe. Though I dare not presume to hope of much success, in any attempts against this distraction, after the frustration of the farre greater endeavours of multitudes that have attempted it with farre greater advantage, yet I have resolved by the help of Christ, to bear witness against the sinne of the Dividers, and leave my testimony on record to posterity, that if it may not excite some others to the work, yet at least it may let them know, that all were not void of Desires for Peace in this contentious age."

This is manifestly written in a mood of sharp disappointment. It is a confession of defeat for a cause that deserves to win. Yet the closing sentence is a stirring testimony and appeal to later generations. The advocates of ecumenical Christianity were frustrated and grieved, but not despairful. There would come other generations in which the ineffectual minority would be a convinced majority, and Christ's prayer for unity would be manifestly in process of fulfillment. We today begin to reap the fruits of the invincible faith of such men as Baxter, " true catholics " who refused to renounce the temporarily defeated cause of Christian unity.

One could assemble a substantial library of treatises containing proposals for Church union, mutual recognition and intercommunion, written in the seventeenth and eighteenth centuries. These deserve a great deal more attention from historians than they have received. They should be studied, not merely for the variations in the methods proposed, but as records of a valiant band of pioneers in ecclesiastical idealism. The time will come when Protestants will realize that these men were truer and profounder interpreters than those who defended denominational segments of the faith. A careful attention to the Reformation sources will reveal that its deeper meaning is unitive and universal rather than particularistic. It is this that is being demonstrated in the ecumenical movement of this century. Although some tend to think of this movement as something new and strange, even as a negation of Protestantism, it is actually an affirmation and fulfillment of the Reformation spirit. If Protestantism were in essence a disorderly assemblage of armed sects, we should do well to desert it for almost any religious camp.

The collection of treatises suggested above would contain the weighty *Irenicum* of David Pareus of Heidelberg (1614); *The Peace of the Church* (1616) by "Rupert Meldenius" (Peter Meiderlin), inventor of the slogan, "In things necessary, unity; in things not necessary, liberty; in all things, charity"; the notably able *Irenicum* of John Forbes (1629); as well as works and letters of G. W. von Liebniz the philosopher and of William Wake, archbishop of Canterbury; and the *Pacific Address to the Protestants* (1720) of Christian Pfaff of Tübingen. The sheer bulk of such treatises is impressive. In 1723 there appeared a printed list of about 150 titles of discussions of Lutheran-Reformed unity, nearly all of which had been published within the previous three years. Decade by decade countless writers took up the theme of a future union of Churches, and no generation was allowed to forget it.

IV

One main point of resistance to unitive effort lay in the persistent rejection by Lutheran churches of projects of union advanced by the Reformed. Many Lutherans deplored this policy, but it was not reversed. Modern Lutheran scholars have offered uncontroversial explanations of this traditional attitude, and of its persistence in some degree to the present time. Lutherans have insisted upon complete doctrinal agreement (*consensus de doctrina evangelii et de administratione sacramentorum,* Augsburg Confession, vii) as the necessary condition of intercommunion. Hermann Sasse, in *Here We Stand,* defends this traditional Lutheran refusal of Reformed advances. In this Lutherans have acted, he says, not on cultural, racial, or national motives, but on doctrinal grounds alone. He somewhat impatiently declares that for four hundred years they have been confronted with an ultimatum: "Let the Lutherans declare at last that they are ready to introduce altar fellowship with the Reformed." He represents this as a demand renewed in each crisis of politics or persecution, with a view to forming a common front against a common foe. The resistance of Lutheranism is thus resistance to temptation, the temptation to compromise through fear of danger. To many, including some Lutherans, this explanation may not seem adequate, but it ought not to be surprising, or to be dismissed as insincere. Lutherans have always guarded the inviolability of their official doctrinal statements. The Formula of Concord adopted by German Lutherans in 1580 judges Luther's catechisms to be "in a sense the Bible of the laity," and regards its own articles on the Lord's Supper as terms of communion (X:5). Jacob Andreae in 1585 refused the right hand of fellowship proffered by Beza, as Luther in 1529 had refused the hand of Zwingli. We make a mistake when we attribute these dramatic repulses to petulance and not to principle. "My faith is at stake," a young Lutheran once said to me, with manifest emotion, when these matters were recalled. The occasional outcropping of mutual intolerance and bitterness and a frequent unwillingness to co-operate even where intercommunion is not an issue are more difficult to excuse.

The Lutheran-Reformed issue was in frequent discussion in the seventeenth century. George Calixtus wrote a partly historical treatise about it, *The Way to Peace Among Protestants,* and from the Reformed side we have a notable little book to the same purpose: *On Agreement and Disagreement of the Reformed with the Brethren of the Augsburg Confession* (1697), by the Geneva theologian, Benedict Pictet. In an urgent preface, Pictet exhorts the Lutherans. We both have, he says, the same God and the same Scripture, reject the same heresies, assent alike to the ancient creeds and the first four ecumenical councils.

"What, then, separates us? Why do we turn the trumpet of Zion into the clarion of Mars? . . . Why should brethren fall by mutual wounds? . . .

I adjure you all by the tender mercies of God and by the precious blood
of his only Son, that you render peace to the Protestant world. Let
the names ' Lutheran ' and ' Calvinist ' be blotted out; let altar no longer
be set over against altar. Eagerly we offer you communion . . . nay,
we entreat you. O happy day when your churches and ours shall spring
to each other's embrace, and joining hands and hearts we shall come
together into one body — with the blessing of God, the applause of
angels, and the rejoicings of saints! "

The two treatises of Calixtus and Pictet were reprinted and may
be read in one volume (Helmstadt, 1700). But they were without
traceable effect upon ecclesiastical policies. They witness to the realization by their authors not only of the undesirability of separation
but of " mutual wounds," alienation, and prejudice. One of the
favorite words used in such appeals in that period is " pacification."
Quarrels between the communions and quarrels within them, seemed
unending. Controversies were to be allayed as a condition of the
negotiation of fraternal unity. All too frequently the honest and
pious seeker of Christian union was denounced as a traitor to denominational tradition. We have outgrown to a large degree this habit
of mind; but we have outgrown it slowly.

V

The Christian consciousness is never detached from the common
social experiences of mankind: it merely appropriates these experiences in its own way. Luke had to begin the gospel story with the
wholly secular information: " In those days a decree went out from
Caesar Augustus that all the world should be enrolled." " The whole
oikoumene ": so the Roman Empire was described, being pre-
sumably thought of as, for practical purposes, as far-flung as the
dwelling places of man. The word " ecumenical " has this sense of
geographic plenitude. It is idle to minimize human geography in
the conception of ecumenicity. The fact that the word " ecumenical "
was applied to the early general councils is not unconnected with
the idea that they were general in a geographical sense. The provinces of the whole Church were represented in them. " Ecumenical "

is a difficult word for the uneducated, and to the fastidious theologian it may seem too secular. But it expresses well the world mission laid upon the heart of the New Testament Church. God " made . . . every nation of men to live on all the face of the earth," and where man dwells, the Church will go. The Christian Church was born geography-conscious, and would be content with no less than a total expansion as wide as the human occupation of the world and a total unity therein (" *ut omnes unum sint,*" " *in universum mundum* ").

The expression " the ecumenical movement " is of recent adoption. It was only in 1936, according to Leonard Hodgson, that a " Faith and Order " document first used the phrase. This date, however, is of no special significance for the movement itself. If we regard the men of ecumenical spirit to whom we have called attention as its forerunners and not its founders, we must look for its real beginnings in the great psychological changes that affected Christians and churches in the eighteenth century. The conception of a world mission became vital in Protestantism through the activity of the Halle Pietists from 1705. The races of the world were still quite inadequately known to Europeans. Later in the century the story of the voyages of Captain James Cook (d. 1779) in the Pacific aroused in Britain an intense popular interest in far and strange peoples. The Evangelical Revival was then in full tide. Its leaders too took the whole globe as their field of action. Yet Wesley saw so many seeming improbabilities in Cook's *Voyages* that he pronounced the story fiction " like *Robinson Crusoe.*" A lad named William Carey, however, on reading the book, associated the new world of exploration with the call of the gospel. He was to make a new beginning of Christian missions. As the missionary movement grew, he proposed (1810) an annual conference in Cape Town of missionaries from all fields to co-ordinate and energize the evangelical missions.

It was inevitable that this idea would suggest itself to others and take other forms. When Alexander Duff, Scottish missionary stationed in Calcutta, visited Philadelphia in February, 1854, his sponsors resolved to hold " a General Missionary Conference," and this led to the " Union Missionary Convention " that met in Broadway

Tabernacle, New York City, the following May. At this convention
Dr. Duff delivered a vigorous public address, in the course of which
he ascribed the idea of the gathering to "the teeming mind of a
citizen of Philadelphia — a layman too — who has a soul great
enough to embrace the whole world — Mr. George H. Stuart." I
quote this, lest the great-souled layman be forgotten. Duff rejoiced
with his enthusiastic hearers in the victory over "narrowness,
bigotry, and exclusiveness," and the growth of brotherly love, that
marked the occasion.

The scene is reminiscent of another that had taken place at the
founding of the London Missionary Society, with interdenomina-
tional support, in 1795, where, amid a storm of applause from a
vast assemblage, David Bogue exclaimed: "Behold us here assembled
with one accord to attend the funeral of bigotry!" Such was the
spirit of evangelical missions, and of the early modern missionary
movement. In this spirit denominational rivalries on mission fields
were minimized, and ultimately methods of co-operation and comity
were developed. In 1838 the American Board of Commissioners for
Foreign Missions undertook to consult with missionaries who had
preceded in any field where work was to be opened. But "bigotry"
did not perish overnight. Opposition to co-operation asserted itself.
The stress of rivalry was felt, and grave conflicts seemed to impend.
It was not until the so-called Centenary Conference of Protestant
Missions, London, 1888, that comprehensive proposals for comity
were first advanced. From comity, or the denominational division
of territory, men went on to think of unity, and to institute plans
for bringing together indigenous churches of different origin.

Already the missionaries were being urged toward union by their
own converts. "They say plainly," one speaker reported at this conference, "it is you foreigners that keep us apart." The repercussions
within the sending communions of this reaction on the field must
be regarded as a significant element in the ecumenical education of
Western Churches. The historical point at which this can best be
observed is the seventh World Missionary Conference held at Edinburgh in 1910. This epochal meeting received searching reports

from eight commissions, one of which dealt explicitly with the problem of unity and division. Recognizing that the Church was to "face a mighty conflict," the Conference found "a real unity of aim underlying" outward differences and separation, while the Christian testimony to the world was weakened by its divisions. The object of missionary effort should be to plant in each land not sects but one united Church of Christ. The Conference in settling a policy for missions was challenging the Churches. It had importance too for the profound impression made upon young men who were to become eminent ecumenical leaders, among them William Temple, Charles Brent, and Nathan Söderblom. It was also partly because Edinburgh, 1910, projected its influence by means of a dozen special committees that something was here done to the Protestant Churches which would not be undone.

VI

Another factor leading to the present movement was the Evangelical Alliance, an association first conceived in Scotland and formed by meetings in Liverpool, 1845, and London, 1846, the object of which was to testify "that a living and everlasting union binds all the believers together in the fellowship of the Church." The Alliance adopted a somewhat conservative set of beliefs, not intended as a confession or creed. It held world conferences at irregular intervals of years and published the addresses delivered at these. It was designed not to negotiate unions but to express the views of its members and to record the information they contributed from their various corners of the world. It was greatly interested in religious liberty, especially as this was associated with evangelical propaganda, and it induced many churches to join in an annual week of prayer at New Year. Adopting the old motto of Rupert Meldenius, "In things necessary, unity; in things not necessary, liberty; in all things, charity," the Evangelical Alliance helped to promote fraternity between leading figures in the different Churches and to develop an all-Protestant consciousness.

It was while the Evangelical Alliance was in process of formation that John Henry Newman passed from Anglicanism to Roman Catholicism. The Alliance was, indeed, something of a protest against the catholicizing efforts of Newman, Pusey, and their associates at Oxford. As we saw above, the Church of England, having suffered secessions to Rome, recovered its stability, and the Oxford Movement went on under the influence of Pusey, who looked toward Anglican union with Eastern and Roman Catholicism.

VII

Amid the numerous proposals for Church co-operation and unity that were put forth in America in the nineteenth century, none was more important than that contained in a book by the Episcopalian William Reed Huntington, *The Church Idea* (1870). The author belonged to a group in the Episcopal Church, led by Bishop W. A. Muhlenberg, that had sought fellowship beyond their own denomination. In his last chapter Huntington calls the Anglican Communion " the church of the reconciliation," and defines its position in four principles " which make the Quadrilateral of pure Anglicanism," and on which he proposes to seek Christian reunion. Discussions that followed led to the adoption by the Episcopal General Convention, meeting in Chicago in 1886, of this Quadrilateral, with a preamble that disclaims any desire to absorb other communions. The Quadrilateral, slightly modified, was adopted by the Lambeth Conference of bishops of 1888. It briefly states belief in the authority of Scripture, the Nicene Creed, the two sacraments, and " the historic episcopate."

The last phrase was to become familiar in subsequent ecumenical discussion, but it has proved surprisingly difficult to clarify. It cannot, in fact, be used as an exact term of discussion, since, historically, the episcopate, even within the Anglican Church, has been different at different times, and has varied widely from any of the forms it assumed in the Church before Constantine. *The Church Review* (New York) in 1890 published a series of interpretations of the Lambeth propositions, to which some non-Anglicans contributed. Among these Charles A. Briggs pointed to the variety of views on the episcopate held within churches practicing it, and proposed, as a Presbyterian, to accept it on the interpretation that it exists *jure humano* and not *jure divino* — in the words of an Ohio bishop, as " not a doctrine but a fact." Bishop W. S. Perry, however, would have none of this interpretation. He stated that as one who voted at both Chicago and Lambeth he was confident that the intention in these meetings was not to countenance any admission of a human origin of the episcopate, but to assert its divine authority and apostolic origin. These papers reflect similar discussions in England at the time.

The first responses to the Lambeth Quadrilateral proved typical of most later learned and popular interpretation. Ecclesiastical convictions are so strong that an objective historical view of the early ministry seems usually to elude even the most learned. The affirmation of the episcopate as " a self-recruiting essential ministry " (in distinction from the presbyterate and the diaconate which are " dependent " upon it) whose duties were " handed on " from the apostles (the language is that of the present bishop of Oxford) has been insistent on the part of High-churchmen. The historical argument for this view has been elaborately presented but has proved convincing only to those disposed to be convinced. The doctrine that the ministry rests upon a divine-right episcopacy has, indeed, a very different history from that of the episcopate itself, and is not shared by all Churches that have bishops. In the Latin Church it has appeared from time to time, but has not been favored by the papacy. The Council of Trent ascribes divine institution not only to bishops but equally to presbyters and deacons, and some of its phrases have been disapproved as " presbyterian " by Anglo-Catholics.

Those who hold episcopacy to be essential to the being of a church are often inclined to regard the doctrine that it is such to be itself a term of communion. Episcopalians who assert this doctrine logically should excommunicate the other Episcopalians who reject it; but in this matter charity triumphs over logic. It is only when approaches are made from nonepiscopal communions that the doctrine is invoked, and the applicants are in effect asked to add to the creed a modern clause: "I believe in the episcopate as of divine institution without which no church exists." Since the episcopate is essential to a church, churches that practice presbyterial ordination are not churches; their presbyters, not being ordained by bishops, are not presbyters, and projects of union with such pseudo churches are betrayals of the *una sancta ecclesia*. These convictions are piously and immovably held, and, on the other hand, rejected with no less sincerity. If they were shared by all members of the Churches in which they appear, they would make impossible all communion and reciprocity between the great families of Churches.

Fortunately Anglicanism as such has made no commitment to this absolute principle. The Lambeth Conference of 1920, indeed, declared for an "equitable approach to union by way of mutual deference to one another's consciences." In later conversations with Free Churchmen (1922) and in the Lambeth documents of 1930, the principle was accepted that in a future union episcopacy should be retained without requirement of "any particular theory as to its origin and character." In this spirit Anglicans have joined in the movement for Church union in South India and entered with two nonepiscopal Churches the Church of South India (1947).

The formation of this Church (1947) marks the most advanced step in corporate union so far taken. It is not without significance that this union has been achieved in an area that was a mission field for numerous denominations. The Indian Churches have gone far ahead of the Churches by whose missionaries they were planted. Yet with few exceptions Western Christians have applauded the step, and regard it as a good omen of union to come for them also. The proposal encountered constant opposition from Anglo-Catholics. In dealing with it, opposing scholars have found new angles of interpretation of the Early Church, so that each side remains fully convinced that it is historically secure. One opponent of the union, Trevor Jalland, proposed as an alternative the immediate adoption of episcopal government by the nonepiscopal Churches and a period of approximation by them to Anglican standards after which their ministry would receive ordination from Anglican bishops. The Church of South India is episcopal, but some of its bishops were formerly nonepiscopal, and no such scheme of probation and absorption as that of Dr. Jalland would in the slightest degree accord with the spirit of the union.

VIII

When Protestants applaud the assertion that no particular doctrine of episcopacy must be required, there is danger of something being overlooked. Any " particular doctrine " of the presbyterate will also have to be left optional. It is time that we asked ourselves not only what was the basic order of ministry in the Early Church, but whether we sincerely intend to imitate or restore it. So much uncertainty remains regarding the historical question that we must either wrangle learnedly or leave one another free to reconstruct it mentally, each as he will. We ought also to face the fact that no present-day Church is at all closely similar in organization to any first century Church. (Very possibly the Disciples of Christ of the American Southwest is *formally* as near to the Early Church in Antioch or in Corinth as any existing communion.) If we read realistically Paul's criticisms of the Corinthians, or the Letters to the Seven Churches in the Apocalypse, we have to acknowledge that first century churches left much to be desired in faith and works. Why should we suppose that the ministry of that age is an indispensable norm for all time to come? Or that lineal succession from its beginners is a *sine qua non* of a valid ministry today? Without the apostolic spirit, succession in an apostolic line of ministers, episcopal or presbyterial, is a delusion. We are in danger of becoming the successors rather of those contentious members of the church at Ephesus who had to be warned not to " occupy themselves with myths and endless genealogies " (I Tim. 1:4). (" The presbyters among you I exhort, who am also a presbyter " — I Peter 5:1.)

Yet it is clear that we cannot come to union by a stultification of our historical judgment, by surrender to those who are unwisely sure. It must be recognized that the doctrine of episcopacy that makes all nonepiscopally ordained ministers in fact laymen will always stand in the way of reunion, and that there can be no repudiation of the reality of ordination where a real pastoral ministry is exercised in Churches seeking union. The only position on which progress toward a united and ecumenical Church is possible is that of a recognition of existing ministries. Historical scholarship has labored the matter long enough to make us sure that to Protestant judgment it will not yield the answers Anglo-Catholics profess to derive from it. The examination of *The Apostolic Ministry* (edited by Kenneth E. Kirk, bishop of Oxford) in *The Reunion of the Church,* by J. E. L. Newbigin, bishop of Madaura, is sufficient to suggest something of the resources available to refute the High-Church historical interpretation, and to show how unimpressive the latter is to scholars of another persuasion. Moreover, South India shows the possibility of genuine reunion in which episcopalians and nonepiscopalians wholeheartedly join on a basis of equality and without mutual humiliation.

In ecumenical literature a great deal has been said about repentance. It is not merely that some have no hope of us unless we repent of a " defective " or " invalid " ministry, but that within the denominations we turn to one another to enjoin repentance for the dismemberment of the Church. But here again discrimination is needful. The dismemberment of the visible Church is, indeed, the common grief of all true Christians. But do many of us really find it possible to " repent " of the origin and existence of our own denomination? It is true that schism is an evil, and that where it has arisen someone has been to blame. But it is far from true that the blame should always rest mainly upon the communion that took a new name. No good will come of an indiscriminate public bewailing of our fathers' sins. It is demonstrable that in many instances denominations were formed by men of excellent intention and deep piety. Some of these men were much less arrogant and more charitable than their opponents — and than their successors. It is for an uncharitable spirit that we should be penitent, and for pharisaic rationalizations of our ecclesiastical superiority. Moreover, it is not, as a rule, by taking flight from our own denomination to any other that we can make a contribution to ecumenical Christianity, but rather by accepting our own Church as a reality and trying to lead it into the world-wide fellowship.

IX

The ecumenical revival of our time involves a revived sense of the significance of the Church in the world, and for the world. It has, however, perhaps by countersuggestion, stirred up each denomination's sense of its own world relationship and world importance. Active world organizations of Presbyterian-and-Reformed, Methodist, Baptist, Congregational, Lutheran, and "Liberal" Churches have followed the beginnings of the Lambeth series of conferences for Anglicanism. While this feeling of denominational ecumenicity seems to counter the progress of the larger movement, it is doubtful if it should be so judged. Ultimate union, if it is to be real, must embrace the values and take over the loyalties of the denominations, and it is well that these should be freshly evaluated. We must make known our inventories to each other: we can share nothing that we have not first appropriated and appreciated. It is likely that in most instances the current revival of the denomination is not promoted in an exclusive spirit.

The view that denominations are, or represent, "sin," a position attributed to the American members of the Lausanne Conference on Faith and Order (1928), has been particularly challenged by Lutherans (cf. Abdel Ross Wentz, "Lutheran Churches and the Modern Ecumenical Movement," in *World Lutheranism Today,* A Tribute to Anders Nygren, pp. 391–417. Stockholm, 1950). Lutheran churches have voiced a desire to secure full consideration of the Protestant confessions and to co-operate denominationally rather than regionally in the World Council of Churches. On this principle the Lutheran World Federation has as one of its purposes: "To foster Lutheran participation in ecumenical movements." The Lutherans are perhaps in danger of taking too high ground against the method of union by "mutual concessions." To express this absolutely is to claim infallibility. But they are justified in objecting to any hasty obliteration of historic denominations and in seeking denominational as well as regional representation on the World Council and its agencies.

Denominations die hard; or, rather, they do not die. Even where their names are abandoned, they carry their typical qualities and procedures into the larger communions formed from them. The participants in any major union are aware in a new way of the value of their own tradition which now contributes significantly to a new and larger whole. They are conscious both of enrichment and of emancipation. The spiritual gain of union lies in this. It is a confluence of streams, a widening of horizons, an increment of resources. In the United Church of Canada many expressed gratification when it was realized that all its members were now associated with the world organizations of Congregationalism, Methodism, and Presbyterianism. With alacrity too, after its formation it rose to action as one Church. Although old denominational habits are still to some extent reflected in its local congregations, it has suffered no crisis traceable to surviving denominationalism. As a Church it has made a selective appropriation of the vital and valuable elements from each of the three Churches that came together in 1925.

X

The list of Church unions achieved in the past century and a quarter, and especially in the last half century, offers ample proof of a strong trend toward the reintegration of broken families of Churches, and exhibits some successes beyond what are usually thought of as "families." World conferences have multiplied in variety and have been increasingly important both for their members and for the Churches represented. These have included world conferences on missions, faith and order, life and work, conferences of Christian youth, and of Christian women. The wars have delayed but not discouraged the movement, and after each of them new forward steps were promptly taken. The plan for the World Council of Churches put forth in 1937 was taken up actively in 1945 and its first assembly was held in Amsterdam, August 23 to September 4, 1948. The literature of the movement has grown to dimensions almost discouraging to the student. Although no popular book has carried it to the non-Christian public, and it has made an inadequate use of radio, the Christian layman has been fairly well supplied with information about its progress. In this way the movement has an advantage over all the efforts of previous centuries toward the same end. Knowledge and discussion of these was too largely confined to an ecclesiastical elite and a few political figures. But there is a great deal yet to be done to acquaint laymen with the movement, and to enlist their informed and spontaneous participation and support.

The ecumenical revival represents the response of Christianity to the challenge of the mechanically unified world. It profits little that we should be able to cover the globe almost instantaneously with propaganda and guided missiles, or to exchange commodities between continents by jet propulsion, if we fail to realize a fellowship of souls that mechanical power shall not disrupt. The political hopes raised by the formation of the United Nations and the economic and educational agencies that stem from it are not to be discounted. But their fulfillment is conditional on the acceptance of fraternal bonds that political action is largely powerless to bring about. The Christian world fellowship, the ecumenical Church, is a thing in itself and exists not merely as a means toward temporal betterment. Yet the world's hope of emergence from chaos and hourly peril lies in the triumph of that spirit which the Church alone propagates. There is no substitute either in humanistic moralism or in the competing religions for the fraternity of the Christian faith.

The non-Christian reader of present-day ecumenical literature will be impressed by two things. He will find Christians at variance on the doctrine of the ministry and on the doctrine of the Eucharist (not to mention other controverted matters) and unable to show emerging solutions of the differences. But if he is fair-minded, he will be not less impressed by the evidence that they refuse to draw iron curtains that shut off discussion, continue to expose themselves to each other's arguments, and often express the hope of ultimate agreement under the leading of the Spirit of God. The association and exchange of theological and practical ideas within the larger portion of world-wide Christianity through the twentieth century era of the raging of the nations and the catastrophes of war; the combination of frankness and brotherly courtesy in this interchange; the basic optimism that underlies it; the enriched concept of the

Church and its mission that emerges from it — these are facts of deep import. They imply a historic magnitude in this movement not to be measured in terms of its organizations, impressive though these are. The fact is not yet fully realized (in secular minds, indeed, quite overlooked) that Christianity itself is unobtrusively taking on a new magnitude in the world, and equipping itself for triumphs to come.

I have called attention to the historic antecedents of the ecumenical movement. But the greatest of mistakes would be to think of it as a mere mechanical structure dealing in the reaffirmation of old dogmas. Through the associations it creates, new life is generated. An impressive proof of the leaven of a fraternal spirit generated within the circle of the movement is seen in the pages of Leon Zander's *Vision and Action,* where a Russian Orthodox writer treats the attitudes of Roman Catholicism, Anglicanism, Protestants, and Orthodoxy alike with penetration, criticism, and sympathy. Dr. Zander exhibits the areas in which unity has not been broken, along with the grave disunity in faith and sacraments. He points frankly to the depressing fact that the prayer for unity is not a common prayer since widely varying notions are present of the unity prayed for. We need first to pray together, " Thy will be done." It is becoming more and more manifest that earnest ecumenical discussion sends men to explore deeper strata of thinking and devotion, where prejudice and bigotry break down.

The ecumenical revival is only beginning. If it continues in mounting strength, it must create an ecclesiastical revolution. The visible church of the future will not be a replica of any Church of the past, or a patchwork of many such. Nor will it be a museum of old theological fragments. Rather, it will be a vital communion of free believers, each aware that he has membership in a holy society and holds communion with innumerable brethren, loyal and beloved, dwelling in every hamlet of the globe, who with him lift up their hearts to God.

Chapter

6

MODERN ROMAN CATHOLICISM

I

In our generation, the Roman Catholic Church has taken on new vigor, especially in English-speaking nations. It commands the obedience and the sincere loyalty of many priests, members of religious orders, and pious lay folk. It employs the services of innumerable well-trained scholars who interpret its principles in the light of modern ideas, and profits by the work of an army of well-qualified popular writers who present its way of life in an attractive light. It expands its institutions and activities. By means of architecture and vestments and ceremonies, it makes itself increasingly visible wherever one goes. It commands a political influence not to be neglected by any nation. It acquires great properties, and prizes social position. In some countries it claims exclusive recognition among religious communions. It is watchfully self-protective and alert to make its critics uncomfortable.

A Roman Catholic historian has described the condition of German Catholicism four hundred years ago as that of "an army in rout." This description is very far from applying to its condition in the world today. Since that era it has suffered many losses and gained many victories. In response to adversaries within and without, it has defined its principles with increasing exactness. In each crisis it has usually, if somewhat tardily, discovered fresh resources to match the danger. It has prized continuity and resisted change, but it has known how to adjust itself to the inevitable without surrendering its fundamental purposes. With accumulated worldly wisdom, and mounting spiritual zest and energy, it has entered the twentieth century and through the distresses of our generation has lived in the spirit of one of its eminent scholars who wrote twenty years ago, " The night is past, the dawn is already here, and Catholic Rome meets the coming age with confidence."

This great institution, comprising about one seventh of the population of the world, provides a part of our environment wherever we are, conditioning the work of other Churches and the lives of their members. Its leaders deplore the fact that other Christians imperil their salvation by remaining outside its fold. Annually a certain number of these others are persuaded to enter it, while the high birth rate of its families insures within it a disproportionately great numerical growth. There is every reason, therefore, that we should accord to it our most serious attention and seek an understanding of the long-time trends within it, and of the role it plays, and seeks to play.

We shall not gain much insight into Roman Catholicism by observing its present-day activities and policies alone. It is true of it, in a greater degree than perhaps of any other institution, that its policies are framed by men deeply conscious of its historical experience, and with distant objectives in view. We shall need to know something of the movements that have stirred it, the decisions and affirmations that have guided it, the humiliations and triumphs, the motives and purposes manifested in its history.

Enfeebled by its long period of decadence, the Church responded weakly to the beginnings and early expansion of the Reformation. There was no little alarm and even bewilderment in high quarters, and counsels were divided. There were those who, like Cardinals Contarini and Sadoleto, desired internal reforms and a moderate policy toward Protestantism, while others, like Cardinal Caraffa, wished to employ the inquisition and other means of compulsion.

The quarter century that elapsed between the December in which Luther burned the pope's bull *Exsurge Domine* (1520) and the December in which the Council of Trent held its first session (1545) was one of disaster to the papacy; but something was already being done to retrieve the disaster. In this interval there arose in Italy a considerable number of new religious fraternities concerned for clerical piety and morals, or engaged in preaching and in works of charity

among the common people. Ignatius Loyola in 1540 became the
founder of the Jesuit order, which more than any other was to direct
and inspire the Counter Reformation. Each of these movements consisted of a small number of very earnest men, conscious of a mission,
anxious to restore discipline and spirituality and to give a new tone
to the Church. At the same time, certain of the greater states of
Europe, adhering to the hierarchal Church and recognizing some
measure of papal authority, maintained within their own dominions
the outward structure of the institution. The simple fact that both
Hapsburg and Valois rulers, traditional enemies and often at war,
alike declined to break from the papacy during the tensions of that
age was of incalculable importance. The defection of either of these
great powers would have imperiled the survival of the papacy itself.

Moreover, under Pope Paul III, 1534–1549, an expectation of serious
reform in the Church had been engendered. In response to a very
widespread demand, a demand often voiced by both Luther and
Erasmus as well as by many others nearer to the papal elbow, Paul
undertook to summon a council. The Councils of Constance and of
Basel in the previous century had affirmed the supremacy of a council over the authority of the pope. The decree *Sacrosancta* enacted at
Constance, April 6, 1415, states that the council has its authority
directly from Christ, and that everybody, including the pope, is
obliged to obey it. This conciliar doctrine had been denounced in
unmeasured terms by Pope Pius II in the bull *Execrabilis* (1460).
But the hope that a reforming council would reform the papacy
had not been extinguished, and had now risen anew in many breasts.
Paul III made anxious preparations for the council, sounding out
Protestant as well as Roman Catholic princes, negotiating warily
with the emperor, and planning matters in advance so as to forestall
any revival of conciliarism and assure the ascendancy of papal
policies.

The pope appointed a fact-finding commission of cardinals in
order to determine, if possible, what were the conditions in the
Church that ought to be reformed. The report of this commission,
presented in February, 1537, was prepared largely by Gasparo Contarini, whose name appears first among its signers. It is a devastating

recital of abuses and scandals. Copies confidentially circulated were soon fed into hungry printing presses in Germany and Italy. This was embarrassing, but salutary. It deepened the concern of good men for reform and revival.

Years before Trent, the rigorous policy of Caraffa was in the ascendant. In 1542, Contarini died. In that year Giovanni Pietro Caraffa, who had been the founder of the Theatine order, induced Pope Paul III to institute a new Court of Inquisition at Rome. The Roman Inquisition, directed by six cardinals, with Caraffa as their presiding officer, proved an effective agency. It sternly suppressed and almost completely uprooted the nascent Protestantism of the Italian cities, though many of its prospective victims managed to escape to other lands.

II

The story of the Council of Trent has often been told by friend and foe. Its most hostile critics have been themselves Roman Catholics, men like the Venetian Paolo Sarpi and the Gallican Guillaume Ranchin. It cannot be treated as a Church assembly apart from the intricate politics and diplomacy of Europe from 1545 to 1563 — from the date of the opening of the Council to the last period of its sessions. The dogmatic decrees and disciplinary canons of the Council of Trent constituted a new platform for the Roman Catholic Church. The Church of the Middle Ages had managed on a much less extensive corpus of explicit dogma. In this long series of utterances, we have in fact a parallel to the numerous Protestant confessions of faith. The typical Protestant doctrines are repudiated and the declared basis of authority is not, as for Protestants, the Scripture alone. On this topic the fathers of Trent (Session 4) affirm a veneration for " the unwritten traditions " received by the apostles from Christ, or dictated to the apostles by the Holy Spirit, which have been preserved in the Catholic Church. These are of equal authority with Scripture. Reformation views of sin and grace, and of justification, are explicitly condemned.

The treatment of penance (Session 14) contains an admirably clear exposition of the medieval doctrine of this sacrament and of its parts: contrition, confession, absolution, and satisfaction. The repetition of penance is supported from Matt. 18:22. To Peter, who had asked whether pardon could be given seven times, our Lord replied: " I say not unto thee, Until seven times: but, Until seventy times seven." Confession should begin as soon as a child is able to discern good from evil. All mortal sins must be confessed. Venial sins may be usefully confessed, but may be omitted without sin, and " expiated by a variety of other means." The more heinous crimes are to be reserved for the judgment of the sovereign pontiff. Priests who are in mortal sin have, nevertheless, the power of binding and loosing.

It was not until twelve years later, in the very last session of the Council, December 4, 1563, that action was taken on the difficult subject of the sale of indulgences. It is stated that the power of conferring indulgences was granted by Christ to the Church and employed in the most ancient times. It is admitted, however, that many abuses and corruptions have crept into the practice of indulgences. The bishops are to investigate these abuses and report them to the provincial synods, after which they may be referred to the sovereign Roman pontiff, who has authority to ordain what may be expedient for the Universal Church.

In the canons and decrees there are few such explicit references as this to the authority of the Roman see. Nevertheless, the position of Rome is carefully guarded. It is noteworthy that the Council adopted the title at the head of its decrees: " The sacred holy ecumenical synod of Trent, lawfully assembled in the Holy Ghost, the legates of the apostolic see presiding therein." The papal legates substituted this style for the old conciliar formula: " *Universalem ecclesiam representantes.*" Thus the authority of the synod is associated with the presiding legates of the pope rather than with the conciliar principle of representation of the entire Church. The membership of the Council of Trent was by no means evenly representative of the Church membership in the various countries. The voting was by numbers, not as at the Council of Constance by nations, and a safe majority of Italians was constantly present.

The authority of bishops was a subject of hot and prolonged de-

bate, the French bishops affirming it strongly in a way that was felt
by the Italians to infringe upon the doctrine of the Roman primacy.
The papal cause against "episcopalism" was ably defended by the
Jesuits present, and was in the main sustained in the formula
adopted. It declares that bishops stand above priests in their power
of confirmation and ordination. They confer orders without consent
or vocation of the people or of the secular power. But it is not
affirmed, as had been proposed, that they hold the power of jurisdiction directly from Christ. Thus, after a perilous encounter, the
advantage went to the papacy. Some ambiguity was left, but the
greatest challenge to papal sovereignty in the Church had been
warded off.

The Council closed; the pope remained. A year later, Pius IV published what was termed "The Profession of the Tridentine Faith,"
which was to serve as a test for ordination. It is a highly condensed
summary of the principal emphases of the decrees of Trent. Two of
its provisions are as follows:

> "V. I embrace and receive all and each of the things which have
> been defined and declared in the Holy Synod of Trent con-
> cerning original sin and justification.
> "IX. [in part] I also affirm that the power of indulgences was left
> by Christ in the Church and that the use of them is most whole-
> some to the Christian people."

I quote still another which expresses a central principle of Roman
Catholicism:

> "X. I acknowledge the Holy, Apostolic, Roman Church as Mother
> and Mistress of all Churches; and to the Roman Pontiff, suc-
> cessor of the blessed Peter, prince of Apostles, and vicar of Jesus
> Christ, I promise and swear true obedience."

This oath has ever since been imposed upon ecclesiastical persons:
a declaration of papal infallibility was added in 1877.

During the sessions of the Council, which claimed in its decisions
the inspiration of the Holy Spirit, the quip was passed around among
the French members that the Holy Ghost came from Rome in a
dispatch box. "I have seen," writes Ranchin, "the original copy of a

letter in the hand of a learned Catholic dated the 19th of May, 1563, written from Trent to Rome by Monsieur de Lansac to Monsieur de Lisle, wherein he entreats him to deal so that the pope would leave the Council to their liberty and send the Holy Ghost no more in a cloke bag." Paul Vergerio, formerly a papal legate in Germany and later a zealous Protestant, afterward wrote to the bishops of Italy that both Paul III and Julius III had sent to the Council ready-made ordinances and decrees with injunctions that nothing should be determined contrary to them. "Whence it came to pass," says Vergerio, "that they commonly say nowadays the Holy Ghost came to Trent packed up in a cloke bag." (I am using the translation of Ranchin by G. Langbaine. *A Review of the Council of Trent,* p. 48. Oxford, 1638.)

III

The contribution of the Jesuit order to the Counter Reformation was incalculable. Cardinal Caraffa saw the possibilities of the order, but feared that its growing power might one day challenge that of the pope. When he became Pope Paul IV, 1555-1559, he sought to lay restrictions upon the Jesuits. They were required to perform routine choir services and asked to elect a new general once in every three years. Diego Laynez, the successor of Saint Ignatius as general of the order, was summarily commanded to institute these highly unwelcome reforms. They accepted the choir services, although the work they wished to do was seriously hampered thereby. As Father James Brodrick remarks, "They did their best and kept cheerful, remembering the pope's great age." When he died at the age of eighty-four, Laynez was summoned to his bedside while the Pope expressed remorse for his policy, professed his love for the society, and presented the general with a coffer full of money for the endowment of a Jesuit College at Rome. (This account of Paul IV's death is reported by Father Brodrick from Father Oliver Manare, a contemporary Flemish Jesuit then living in Rome. Brodrick regards him, however, as "not a particularly exact or critical writer." *The Progress of the Jesuits, 1556–79,* p. 31. London, 1946.)

Whatever dying thoughts Pope Paul IV had regarding the Jesuits, the society did not deserve his hostility. In the later sessions of the Council of Trent, Laynez himself, with his colleague, Alphonso Salmeron, participated very effectively in the debates and uniformly supported the papal interests. Spanish and French bishops in the Council were advocating a high doctrine of episcopal authority which the papal legates thought dangerous. The issue was in hot debate over a period of about nine months, and Laynez, despite the fact that he was crippled with arthritis, bore the brunt of the fight. He fought, says Brodrick, " for the rights of the Holy See during those stormy months as he had never fought before."

In the early months of the Council a proposal had been adopted that a catechism be prepared for the instruction of children and lay people. Progress on this project was delayed until near the end, and it was left unfinished when the Council closed. The committee appointed by the legates to prepare it brought back a labored treatise intended for the use of priests in their pastoral labors. Protestantism had been promoted by catechisms for the common folk. In the previous decade, the Jesuit apostle Peter Canisius (d. 1597) had prepared a *Summa,* a " Shorter," and a " Shortest " Catechism, the last of which, a very simple statement, was already vastly popular when the Tridentine Catechism appeared. Saint Charles Borromeo had much to do with the completion of the new catechism. After careful revision it was published about the end of the year 1566 under Pope Pius V. The best English translation is that of John A. McHugh and Charles J. Callan: *Catechism of the Council of Trent for Parish Priests,* New York and London, 1923. The catechism is a document of first importance for our understanding of the Counter Reformation. Completely faithful to the teachings of Trent, it expresses these amply, simply, and persuasively. It has not the advantage of brevity. The translation occupies 589 pages. Though called a catechism, it is not couched in the form of question and answer, but of continuous discourse with paragraph headings. Like many short medieval handbooks, it treats in turn the Creed, the Sacraments, the Commandments, and the Lord's Prayer. We find within it many admirable expressions of true Christian piety. The section on prayer is particularly replete with these. One who reads it over will find himself becoming familiar with the sources of the finer types of lay piety in modern Roman Catholicism. Take, for example, this:

"We are to pray for all mankind, without exception of enemies, nation, or religion; for every man, be he enemy, stranger, or infidel, is our neighbor, whom God commands us to love and for whom, therefore, we should discharge a duty of love which is prayer. To the discharge of this duty, the apostle exhorts when he says: I desire that prayer be made for all men. In such prayers, we should first ask for those things that concern spiritual interest, and next for what pertains to temporal welfare."

There are naturally a great many statements not so acceptable as the above to Christians of other communions. The authors of the catechism were careful to affirm in unmistakable terms the supremacy of the Roman pontiff. The explanation of the Sacrament of Orders contains statements on the degrees of the priesthood, under the headings " priests," " bishops," " archbishops," " patriarchs," " the pope." In the last of these we read:

"Above all these [patriarchs] the Catholic Church has always placed the Supreme Pontiff of Rome, whom Cyril of Alexandria in the Council of Ephesus named the chief bishop, father, and patriarch of the whole world. He sits in that chair of Peter in which, beyond every shadow of doubt, the prince of the apostles sat until the end of his days, and hence it is in him that the Church recognizes the highest degree of dignity and a universality of jurisdiction, derived, not from the decrees of men or councils, but from God himself; therefore, he is the father and guide of all the faithful, of all the bishops, and of all the prelates, no matter how high their office, and as successor of Saint Peter, as true and lawful vicar of Christ our Lord, he governs the Universal Church."

In the treatment of the Decalogue, the First and Second Commandments according to the numbering of Reformed and Anglican Churches are, of course, combined as the First Commandment, and our Tenth Commandment is divided into Ninth and Tenth, with the intervening numbers corresponding to this arrangement. The words, " Thou shalt not make to thyself a graven thing," in what is here the First Commandment, are interpreted very freely, and the employment of pictures to represent attributes of God is justified from the figure of the Ancient of Days in Daniel and the Scriptural reference to the dove as a form taken by the Holy Ghost. So the Commandment is said not to forbid representation of the divine persons, of angels and of saints. It is alleged that this position is confirmed by the monuments of the apostolic age, the general councils, and the writings of many of the Fathers. On the topic of the invocation of the Virgin Mary, it is stated that

" we piously and humbly fly to her patronage in order that by her intercession she may reconcile God to us sinners, and may obtain for us those blessings which we stand in need of in this life and in the life to come."

I shall later refer to the modern cult of Mary. It is sufficient to observe now that the direction here given to Roman Catholic piety quite frankly reaffirms medieval against Reformation principles, and interprets the Scriptures accordingly.

The most ardent champions of reform and agents for the revitalization of the Church in the latter half of the sixteenth century were members of the Jesuit order. Through this period, the labors of Peter Canisius, chiefly in German-speaking areas, constitute an impressive lesson in constancy and zeal. Nothing in this apostolate was more important than the planting of a chain of Jesuit colleges in Germany, Austria, and Bohemia. These supplied intellectual strength and permanence to the Counter Reformation movement. Many members of the order undertook perilous missions in Protestant territories, while others were engaged in efforts to convert non-Christians in distant lands. Besides the Jesuits, many orders and agencies were now at work restoring the inner life and structural firmness of the Church. Not all the abuses were eliminated. The selling of indulgences, for example, while greatly reduced, did not cease. But as compared with conditions at the beginning of the sixteenth century, the end of it witnessed a vast improvement in earnestness and religious reality. The advance of Protestantism was checked. In some nations as in Italy, Spain, and Poland, an incipient Protestantism had been crushed and almost exterminated, and its outlook in France,

Hungary, and Bohemia was bleak indeed. Those who had expected the papacy to be extinguished, and those who had hoped to see it subordinated to a Church council, were doomed to disappointment.

IV

Painful, certainly, have been the adjustments of the Roman Catholic Church to the modern national spirit. Europe was to remain permanently divided in religion, and the so-called wars of religion were to mingle with national struggles. France, indeed, had its civil war of religion in the sixteenth century. In Germany, the major strife was the Thirty Years' War, 1618-1648. While it is true that in some degree religious differences animated the contestants in these bitter conflicts, it should be remembered that long before the Reformation, and in the decades just preceding it, parts of Europe were constantly bleeding from war, although these earlier conflicts were in general not animated by religion at all. The motives that make for war are manifold and in Europe they have been almost constantly present.

In the Peace of Westphalia at the end of the Thirty Years' War, the papacy suffered political humiliation. Trautmannsdorf, the representative of Emperor Ferdinand III of Austria, did not hesitate to bargain away Church property regardless of the claims of Pope Innocent X, and agreed to numerous concessions to Protestants. The popes thereafter were more than ever embarrassed in their relations with the nations. It was evident that the nominal adherence of a ruler to the papacy offered little assurance of any international championing of the papal interests. This indifference on the part of Roman Catholic Governments to the political policies of the Vatican has many subsequent illustrations. All the major postwar political settlements since the Reformation have been very unsatisfactory to the popes. Thus Pope Paul IV vigorously condemned the peace of Augsburg, 1555, and was deeply aggrieved at Charles V, and especially his brother Ferdinand, for their acceptance of clauses in that treaty that countered papal claims. The Peace of Westphalia contained a provision nullifying in advance any protest that might be made by the pope. But the ambassador, Chigi, and later Pope Innocent X himself, protested vigorously. In the brief, *Zelo domus Dei,* Innocent X expresses indignation that the Lutherans are allowed the free exercise of their heresy and that other things are agreed upon prejudicial to the Roman see. The articles of peace were declared null and void. They were not to be observed even though fortified by an oath. This protest, the pope adds, shall remain valid for all time. The Peace of 1815 was scarcely more agreeable to Pius VII. It is well known that Benedict XV sought in vain papal representation at the peace table after World War I, and that the pope is not represented in the United Nations organization. Whatever influence the popes may have in the framing of political policies is for the most part exercised otherwise than by participation in international organizations and through the ordinary channels of diplomacy.

The spirit of nationalism has also profoundly affected the internal life of the Roman Catholic Church in many countries. The most striking illustration of this is seen in the history of Gallicanism. From the high Middle Ages down, powerful kings of France had sought and acquired a large control of the Church with respect to appointments and taxation. Many concordats, and notably that of 1438, which affirmed the principle of conciliar government, had been negotiated to regulate relationships between the pontiffs and the French monarchy. The conciliar principle was dropped in the Bologna Concordat of 1516, which left appointments to the episcopate and to abbacies in France largely in the control of the king. In the seventeenth century, French Gallicanism moved on to a new stage. The great prelates who owed their appointments to Louis XIV could be counted upon to support the king's decisions. They stood by him when he undertook to extend his regalian rights in southern France, although this involved a dire quarrel with Pope Innocent XI. It was no other than Jacques Bénigne Bossuet, perhaps the greatest ecclesiastic of his century, who in the king's interest drew up the Declaration of the Clergy of France, 1682. It denies that kings are subject to ecclesiastical authority in temporal things, but on the other hand it affirms the continued validity of the decree *Sacrosancta* of the Council of Constance by which the pope was subjected to the Council. The pope's decision, it is said, is final only after the Church has given its consent. Innocent now refused to acquiesce in the consecration of the bishops who had been, according to the custom, appointed by Louis, and Louis in turn seized Avignon and appealed for a general council of the Church. About ten years later the conflict ended in a compromise. But the spirit of Gallicanism lived on into the nineteenth century. It may be said to have reached its culmination in the measures taken by Napoleon in the Concordat of 1801, by which Roman Catholicism was held to be " the religion of the majority of Frenchmen," and bishops were to be appointed by nomination of the Government and canonically instituted by authority of the pope. The Church property was taken over and clergy were put on stated salaries.

Febronianism is the name often applied on German and Austrian soil to the phenomenon corresponding to Gallicanism. It is derived from the pseudonym " Justinus Febronius" assumed by Nicholas von Hontheim, bishop of Treves, who in 1763 published his cele- brated book, *On the State of the Church and the Power of the Roman Pontiff*. He asserted conciliar against papal claims and applied in a nationalist sense the old conciliar doctrines of authority. Numerous German bishops adhered to the teachings of Febronius, and his in- fluence was strongly felt in the ecclesiastical policies of Joseph II of Austria, 1765–1790.

The humiliations administered to Pope Pius VII by Napoleon called forth widespread sympathy for the papacy, and in the settle- ment of 1815 an effort, on the whole unsuccessful, was made to re- store the papal political prestige. Meanwhile in May, 1814, Pope Pius VII had re-entered Rome and issued the bull *Sollicitudo omnium* by which the Jesuit order was restored. Pius and his suc- cessor, Leo XII, repeatedly condemned Protestant Bible societies; and Leo set the Jews of Rome again in a ghetto, from which they were released by Pius IX in 1846.

Pius IX (1846–1878) and four of his successors dramatized their protest against the treatment of them by the Italian State in 1871 by regarding themselves as prisoners in the Vatican. The imprisonment ended with the Vatican Treaty of 1929 between Mussolini and Pius XI. This pontiff was so fascinated by the dictator that he more than

once referred to him in public as " a man sent by divine providence."
Catholic political parties opposing Mussolini were peremptorily or-
dered by the pope to dissolve. But Mussolini gave the Vatican many
anxious hours before the beginning of World War II.

V

Nineteenth century ultramontanism first found explicit utterance
in the works of two French noblemen who had suffered from the
violence of the revolution, Louis Gabriel Ambroise, Vicomte de
Bonald, and Joseph Marie, Comte de Maistre. De Bonald wrote in
1796 a three-volume work entitled *Theory of Political and Religious
Power in Civil Society,* and De Maistre hailed him as a brother.
De Maistre's impressive book, *Du pape,* appeared in 1817. These
writers, looking upon the Revolution as satanic, set forth a romantic
view of the papacy in history as the principal agency of civilization
and unity. In the historical troubles of Europe the popes were the
peacemakers and mediators. Gallicanism is wholly repudiated; religion and culture are now to be centered in the papacy, and human-
ity to enjoy peace and welfare under a papal theocracy.

Many eminent Roman Catholic writers took up this theme. It was
combated, however, by a group of " Liberal Catholics," who desired
to see the Church brought into more favorable relations with the
political liberalism that was then arising to challenge the reactionary
Governments. Certain of these, " the pilgrims of liberty," personally
visited and appealed to Pope Gregory XVI in 1831, who responded
a year later in his encyclical *Mirari vos* (August 15, 1832), roundly
condemning modern impiety and liberalism. Gregory described the
view that every man has a claim to liberty as " an insane idea " and
" a pernicious error." But a far greater furor was created when Pius
IX issued his bull, *Quanta cura,* of December 8, 1864, which contained the celebrated Syllabus of Errors. It would appear that the
idea of publishing an authoritative list of errors was suggested by
the young man who was later to be Pope Leo XIII. The Syllabus
lists eighty statements for condemnation. It is an error that " the
Roman pontiff and ecumenical councils have exceeded the limits of

their power, have usurped the rights of princes and have committed errors in defining matters of faith and morals." It is an error that "the Church ought to be separated from the State and the State from the Church." It is an error to object to the exclusive claims of Roman Catholicism in the State (77), or to claim the opportunity of worship for non-Roman Catholic immigrants into Roman Catholic countries (78). And the final error is "that the Roman pontiff can and ought to reconcile himself to and agree with progress, liberalism, and up-to-date civilization" (*cum recenti civilitate*).

Pope Pius was already preparing an assembly for the declaration of the dogma of infallibility, a doctrine that had been held by many, rejected by many, and probably neglected by most Roman Catholics until the rise of ultramontanism. It may have been the pressure of secular Italian nationalism that called forth from Pius and his supporters the determination to press for the affirmation of the dogma. Many true believers in infallibility thought the time inopportune for declaring it. While French troops temporarily held off Victor Emmanuel from gaining control of Rome, final preparations were made for the Vatican Council, and it opened on December 2, 1869. The Pope assumed the right to initiate all proposals. A minority, surprising in number, resisted for a time the pressure for the declaration of infallibility. On July 18, 1870, many of the opposition having departed in despair, the decree *Pastor aeternus,* which embodied the doctrine was adopted. The essential passage is:

"We, with the approval of the sacred council, teach and define that it is a dogma divinely revealed that when the Roman pontiff speaks ex cathedra, that is, when discharging the office of shepherd and doctor of all Christians in virtue of his supreme apostolic authority to define the doctrine to be held by the Universal Church concerning faith and morals, he enjoys, by divine assistance promised to him in the blessed Peter, that infallibility by which the divine Redeemer willed his Church to be endowed in the definition of doctrine concerning faith and morals. And therefore, such definitions of the Roman pontiff are irreformable of themselves and not by virtue of the consent of the Church. Whoever shall presume to contradict this our definition, which God forbid, let him be anathema."

It is further taught that the Roman Church exercises an episcopal power over all other Churches and that this power is "immediate." Clergy and laity must subordinate themselves to it. This disposes of any remnant of episcopal autonomy left by the Council of Trent. But what is "the infallibility with which Christ willed to endow his Church"? Has any pope since 1870 made an utterance that can be characterized as infallible? No theologian can point with certainty to such an utterance. On the explanations given, infallibility becomes something intangible. We can perhaps safely associate the notion of infallibility with the declaration of a new dogma; but this was done in 1950 without special reference to the infallibility decree. So little is it a basis of argument that one might almost compare it with the doctrine of sinless perfection where no instance of this attainment is specified. Probably there are many Roman Catholics who take a certain comfort from the assurance that they have an infallible head of the Church; but I suspect that the doctrine of papal infallibility has given more concern to Protestants than to Roman Catholics and aroused among them a greater interest. If the papacy has risen in the estimation of the world since the days of Pius IX, it is not because of the assertion of this doctrine, but because of the greater personal dignity and eminence of some of the popes of the later period.

VI

So fascinating is the story of the papacy in its political and diplomatic relationships that we too readily forget the religious life of Roman Catholicism, its saints, its prayers, its devotional literature, and all the spiritual food by which it is nourished. The history of Protestantism has often been likewise treated with little reference to the story of its devotional aspects. Essential to the Jesuit order was a profound examination, and an unrelenting discipline, of the interior life. Asceticism of the body was disregarded save in the matter of reducing the body to efficiency in the service of religion, while the asceticism of the spirit and the training of the will were intensified. Salvation is not so much by faith as by the right direction of the will. Loyola believed that the will of man was not helpless to do good. Against the Augustinians and the Reformers, who stressed the inability of man, the Jesuits affirmed the freedom of the will, together with the principle of obedience. Early in their history they became the spiritual guides of innumerable persons, many of them of considerable social distinction. As directors of souls they accumulated a great lore of casuistry which survives in a vast number of treatises of that era.

It was in seventeenth century France that Roman Catholic piety attained its highest level. In 1686 a devout French author, Étienne Molinier, wrote:

" Never in the world has there been so full a knowledge of divine mysteries, never such full explanations of Scripture, such illumination of theology, such clearing away of difficulties, such manifestations of truth; never such a multitude of theologians, casuists, contemplatives, and spiritual masters, opening by voice or by ink, by flesh or spirit, so many windows toward heaven."

This passage is quoted by Henri Brémond, the able historian of the French literature of devotion, whose *Histoire littéraire du sentiment religieux en France* (1916–1933) fills eleven ample volumes. Brémond states that he has excluded from his survey an immense heap of " rubbish." He treats with enthusiasm the still vast treasury of devotional writing that exhibits high quality. " Devout humanism " is Brémond's term to describe what he prizes most of this material. The French Church possessed many men of wide reading and excellent talents for writing, who made themselves experts in the direction of souls, some of whom still speak helpfully to those seeking spiritual guidance. This was the age of Pierre de Bérulle (d. 1629), founder of the French congregation of the Oratory (1611), a great inspirer of spirituality; of the ardent Saint Francis de Sales (d. 1622), author of the *Introduction to the Devout Life* (1609); of François de la Mothe Fénelon (d. 1715), director of courtly ladies and military men, teacher of " recollectedness " or spiritual composure amid distractions, and of " *bonne volonté*," which for him meant willing obedience to the commands of God; the age of Jacques

Bénigne Bossuet (d. 1704), prelate, orator, historian, theologian, and, like others here named, author of thousands of spiritual letters. Saint Vincent de Paul (d. 1660), a disciple of Bérulle, stands in the forefront of practical mystics of all time. His wide contacts and travels are reflected in his voluminous spiritual correspondence; and he possessed a peculiar genius for inaugurating and conducting charitable and missionary enterprises. The Sisters of Charity (1618) constituted one of his more important foundations. Saint Vincent, in his attitude to Protestants, rose above the intolerant spirit that was still dominant in his time.

In this period also many sought spiritual attainment in solitude, cultivating a tranquil devotion and contemplation based upon the Psalter rather than the mystical fervor of Saint Bernard or Saint Francis. Spanish mysticism took intense and austere forms, especially in Saint John of the Cross (d. 1591), and flowered in the Quietism of Miguel Molinos (d. 1697).

Another type of piety, which clashed with that of the Jesuits, grew directly out of the intensive study of Saint Augustine by Cornelius Jansen, bishop of Ypres. Jansen's great work entitled *Augustinus* was published in 1640, two years after the author's death. In a long historical introduction Jansen accused the Jesuits of Pelagianism, and called for a return to faith in accordance with the teachings of Augustine and Paul. Certain of the papal decisions seemed to him inconsistent with Augustine's theology. Jansenism was assailed and condemned in several papal utterances, but it attracted numerous devoted supporters. Jansen's personal friend, Jean du Vergier de Hauranne, Abbé de St. Cyran, and Blaise Pascal, one of the greatest minds of a great century, were among those who took up the defense of the work. While at the community of Port Royal near Paris to which numerous Jansenists had come, Pascal wrote his celebrated *Provincial Letters,* 1556-1557, a satirical exposure of the casuistry of the Jesuits and Dominicans. The Gallican Church was torn by the controversy which followed. Many of the clergy refused to obey the bull *Unigenitus* (1713), since it condemned not only the Jansenists but also passages from Augustine and even teachings of Scripture. Through the intervention of Louis XV, the Jansenists were sup-

pressed in France and some of the leaders took refuge in the Nether-
lands. At Utrecht in 1723 they elected a bishop and established an
independent communion. The Netherlands Jansenists became asso-
ciated with the irreconcilable opponents of the Vatican decrees, 1870.
The so-called Old Catholic party which in 1873 became the Old
Catholic Church, received holy orders from the Jansenist bishop of
Deventer in Holland. The Amsterdam conference of the World
Council of Churches (1948) held a session in the Old Catholic
Church at Utrecht.

Jansen had exalted Augustine as the doctor of doctors, while the
Jesuits drew their nurture largely from Aquinas. In the Arminian
controversy within the Reformed Church during the same era, Arminianism corresponds somewhat to the Jesuit position, while the
principles of official Calvinism approximate those of Jansenism. But
while the Jansenists were defeated, the situation was reversed in the
Protestant controversy, in which the Augustinian-Calvinist tradition
was then victorious.

Jansen expounds at great length the argument that man is morally
unable without grace; and for him grace begins from faith in Christ.
Faith is something given, not attained; the easy doctrine of " sufficient grace " presented by the Jesuits is repudiated. The believer's
will is activated by grace. Jansen was anxious to differentiate his
views from those of the Calvinists. In letters, he likened Protestants
to Turks and thought that they deserved more persecution than they
got. Yet there is a broad resemblance of his doctrine to that of Calvin,
and that of Calvin's early seventeenth century followers.

The teachings of the Jansenists exercised a great influence in the
realm of piety. The Port Royalists produced many books. L. Frédéric Jaccard in his excellent monograph on Saint Cyran, speaks of
their books of edification as " innumerable." Their influence upon
the piety of French Protestantism was not negligible. Among these
gifted authors, it is Pascal who alone shines with the light of genius.
His *Thoughts on Religion and Some Other Subjects,* 1670, has fascinated and inspired countless readers. One of Pascal's greatest interpreters was Alexandre Vinet, a nineteenth century Protestant of
great spiritual and intellectual gifts.

Controversies over books of devotion and piety have not been infrequent. It is a field of individualism in which uncensored utterances are apt to escape to the general public, producing ecclesiastical headaches. Celebrated is the case of Madame Jeanne Marie Guyon. She was a pious and precocious child who found herself at eighteen married, through family arrangements, to a rich but ill-grained invalid, and at twenty entered upon the earnest cultivation of the mystical life. She was struck by the words of a Franciscan friend of her father, " You are seeking without what you have within; seek God in your own heart and you will find him." Her Quietism was a devotion to the God within. John Wesley translated her own account of her life, written for Bossuet in 1695, when she was accused of heresy and Bossuet headed a commission to try her.

She wrote with great ease and very extensively. *The Spiritual Torrents* and *The Short and Easy Way of Prayer* were written under the influence of her director, Father la Combe. They reflect the intense experiences that she had known in which, after long anguish, she reached what she called the unitive state. She was a neurotic and erratic person, and being untrained in theology, she made use of phrases that were startling and unorthodox. Her Quietism reached the point of indifference with regard to her own salvation and resembled the teaching of Miguel Molinos, author of *Spiritual Guide,* 1675, who had died in prison, his doctrines having been condemned by Pope Innocent XI at the bidding of Louis XIV. Another highly temperamental Quietist was Antoinette Bourignon (d. 1680) of Lille, who also wrote extensively and whose influence was felt in Protestant Holland and Scotland. Both these women taught the doctrines of extreme Quietism, and both were very excitable and very energetic. The great and wise bishop Fénelon, undertaking to give spiritual direction to Madame Guyon, found himself more directed than director. He so far felt her influence as to introduce into his writings some phrases that had been made familiar by her, and his book *Maxims of the Saints on the Interior Life* showed that many long-approved devotional writers used similar language. Madame Guyon went to prison, and Fénelon to the country. Meanwhile Nicholas Hermann, of Lorraine (Brother Lawrence), a lame veteran who had become a kitchen servant in a Carmelite monastery, in his *Conversations and Letters on the Practice of the Presence of God,* (1666–1691), had given more wholesome expression to the quietistic type of devotion:

" The time of business does not with me differ from the time of prayer and in the noise and clatter of my kitchen, while several persons are calling for different things, I possess God in as great tranquillity as if I were upon my knees at the blessed Sacrament."

VII

But Roman Catholic piety has been of various types. Marguérite Alacoque, a Burgundy nun who had practiced extreme mortifications, conceived of Jesus as her lover and, under the spiritual direction of a Jesuit, witnessed extraordinary visions. In one of these the heart of Jesus was exposed in his body, glowing like the sun, and she was commanded to institute what was called the devotion of the Sacred Heart. Pope Clement XIII, in 1765 authorized this devotion in response to Jesuit appeals, although other orders had opposed it. The Neopolitan Alphonso Maria de Liguori was instrumental in founding the order of Redemptorists (1733). After the Jesuits were expelled from Portugal, France, Spain, Naples and Parma, and then suppressed by Clement XIV in 1773, the Redemptorists succeeded to some of their functions and were very active until the Jesuit order was restored in 1814. Through his writings and teachings Liguori contributed greatly to a revival of ascetic piety. He gave increased currency to the cult of the Virgin Mary, especially through his popular book, *The Glories of Mary* (1750).

With the rise of Ultramontanism in the early nineteenth century, we observe a great deal of attention to the cult of Mary. The Virgin had long been adored, and in popular esteem was held to intercede with Christ himself in belief of sinners. The Catechism of Trent, as we saw, affirmed that she "reconciles God to us." The doctrine of her perpetual virginity was a commonplace of the medieval Church. In the high Middle Ages some writers began to advocate the view of the Immaculate Conception of Mary. The doctrine was strongly opposed by Saint Bernard and was not adopted by Aquinas. It was favored, however, by Franciscan theologians, including Duns Scotus. For ascetic minds, it was a natural corollary of the notion of her sinlessness, which was assumed in connection with the devotions offered to her. Pius IX elevated this widespread belief to the status of an official dogma in the bull *Ineffabilis Deus,* December 8, 1854, which declares:

"The doctrine which holds that the blessed Virgin Mary from the first moment of her conception by a special grace and privilege of Almighty God in virtue of the merits of Christ, was preserved immaculate from all stain of original sin, was revealed by God."

On November 1, 1950, another important addition was made to the body of dogma regarding Mary. In the apostolic constitution, *Munificentissimus Deus,* (Text in *Acta apostolicae sedis,* November 4, 1950), " the bodily assumption of the Blessed Virgin Mary into heaven " was " defined as a dogma of divine and Catholic faith " by Pope Pius XII. Modern Mariolatry has cherished the legend of the Assumption of Mary, which early in the Middle Ages found a place in popular piety and a recognition in some liturgical forms. The authoritative affirmation that Mary's body was in actual historical fact resurrected and raised to heaven might seem to call for support from historical testimony. But no witnesses of the event, or early attestations of it, are cited by the pope. The identification made by some scholastics (and their present-day followers) of the blessed Virgin with the " woman clothed with the sun " — the portent that " appeared in heaven " — is noted, however, together with other passages of Scripture (Gen. 3:15; Isa. 7:14; Luke 1:26–38). The argument from Rev., ch. 12, is that the author of the Apocalypse, presumed to be the apostle John, saw Mary in heaven. (See the article by Dominic Ungar: " Did St. John See Mary in Glory? " *Catholic Biblical Quarterly,* XII, 1950, pp. 405 ff.) But the passage seems frail evidence indeed for the dogma.

Thus, by recent popes Mary, mother of Jesus, is being deified in official dogmatic pronouncements which affirm her miraculous entrance into human life and her miraculous departure to heaven. " We have also," says Pope Pius, " placed our pontificate under the special patronage of the Holy Virgin." The new dogma appears utterly indefensible from the standpoint of historical documentation. It is remarkable, indeed, that no real effort is made to prove the alleged historical fact by historical evidence. The underlying reason for regarding it as true seems rather to be the fact that it has been believed by many of the faithful. The promulgation of the dogma was prepared for by various formal acts, and attended by ceremonies that gave it all the solemnity possible. It was the work of the pope on the advice of bishops, and appears to be an ex-cathedra utterance concerning faith, and thus to be " infallible " in the sense of the Vatican decree. Indeed it carries a warning like an anathema: " If anyone counters it, he will incur the indignation of Almighty God and the Blessed Apostles, Peter and Paul."

What effect this pronouncement may ultimately have upon the Roman communion it is impossible to foresee. The suggestion has been made in secular journals that the dogma will be accepted by intellectuals as legend or poetry. Certainly no freedom to interpret it thus is implied. We can hardly doubt that its tendency is to alienate some admirers of the Church from without, and to discourage those who have sought a Roman-Anglican *rapprochement*. The earlier protest of the Anglican archbishops against the proposed declaration of the dogma, and various subsequent Protestant statements on it, indicate that it has distressed many Christians both as a fresh occasion of division and as a concession to obscurantism. Coming with great solemnity from a very great Church, it may tend to bring derision upon the Christian faith.

Pope Leo XIII (1878–1903) did his utmost to cultivate in the Church new theological learning and an interest in social questions. His encyclical *Rerum novarum*, May 15, 1891, which is perhaps the finest masterpiece of all his utterances, laid down, in opposition to Marxian socialism, principles for solutions of modern economic problems in essential accord with the teachings of Thomas Aquinas. His *Providentissimus Deus*, November 18, 1893, set forth a plan for the study of the Holy Scriptures. This was to be done by the use of Hebrew and Greek in addition to the Vulgate text which Trent had authorized. He later instituted a commission for Biblical study. Pius X took action to encourage the study of Scripture in the seminaries, Benedict XV, September 15, 1920, quoting Saint Jerome, asserted not only the inspiration but the inerrancy of Scripture, and warned against " insane freedom in ventilating opinions " in Biblical criticism. Pius XII, added, September 30, 1943, a substantial encyclical entitled *Divino afflante Spiritu,* which gives information on the modern progress within Catholicism of studies in this field. The pope here interprets the teaching of Trent on the Scripture, explaining that the authorization of the Vulgate in no way diminishes the value and authority of the original text. He urges the study of Oriental languages and antiquities, and attention to " historical, archaeological, and other auxiliary sciences," but only as a basis for theological and doctrinal teaching. The Pontifical Biblical Commission has given answers to a number of questions that naturally arise in the course of Biblical study. The commission has stated that Moses' authorship of the Pentateuch must be maintained, as also the unity of the prophecy of Isaiah, and the Pauline authorship of Hebrews. Such provisions seriously restrict Roman Catholic Biblical scholarship. There can be no question as to the high competence of many of the Church's scholars and of the growing attention to the Bible in the Roman Catholic schools. The spread of authorized and permitted texts and translations to the common people is a natural outcome of this new activity and Biblical study. Apparently a process has been instituted that may conceivably do much to transform the character of Roman Catholic piety, directing it into Biblical channels. This interesting development comes in marked contrast to the pronouncement of the dogma of the Assumption of Mary.

VIII

The vast losses of the Roman Church at the time of the Reformation were partially recompensed by means of its missionary enterprises in that era. Its recent losses in eastern Europe are largely balanced by gains in some of the most progressive nations of the world. Through much experience and adversity, it has learned institutional wisdom and skill in the promotion of its cause. Its successes often occasion alarm to those who hold evangelical beliefs, and to others not of its fold.

Doubtless many thoughtful Roman Catholics would not endorse without qualification the principle expressed in the Jesuit organ, *Civilta Cattolica,* April, 1948, in the words:

" The Roman Catholic Church, convinced, through its divine prerogative, of being the only true Church, must demand the right of freedom for herself alone, because such a right can only be possessed by truth, never by error."

Yet this affirmation is supported by the weight of tradition, and has been modified in policy only under necessity. In recent years the methods and policies of the Church have been the subject of numerous illuminating adverse analyses by liberal and Protestant writers, while, as always, they have been loyally expounded and defended from within. Although the bitterness and recklessness of mutual charges have certainly been diminished, there is no evidence that the long quarrel is wearing itself out.

Roman Catholicism is like a medieval cathedral, always crumbling and sometimes peppered with cannon shot, always being rebuilt with slightly altered design. It is likely to be quite familiar to our children's children, and to their descendants through long generations. But the reviving forces by which it has benefited have often come from without. And the rivalry of Protestantism is saving it today. Where Protestants are few by comparison, Roman Catholicism does not exhibit its best qualities.

But what of ourselves? There are spots on the map where a people adhering to a single Protestant sect are unenlightened, prejudiced, reactionary, and unjust. In some areas the presence and activity of Roman Catholicism is a useful challenge and stimulus to Protestantism. How often in life we gain incalculably from those who would like to thwart us! We Protestants naturally grow impatient of the tensions that arise from the assertion of Roman Catholic claims in education and community life. Sometimes we regretfully find ourselves under the necessity of resisting hierarchical aggression. But let

us not pray for the extinction of Roman Catholicism. We ought to
reflect that in our own Churches we are prone to complacency and
inertia, and that the stimulus of Roman Catholic pressure may help
to deliver us from the insidious evils that afflict every Church whose
status is unchallenged.

SELECTED BIBLIOGRAPHY

CHAPTER I

Anderson, James, *Memorable Women of Puritan Times*. Two volumes. London, 1862.

Bancroft, Richard, *Dangerous Positions and Proceedings . . . under Pretence of Reformation*. London, 1712.

Baxter, Richard, *The Practical Works of the Reverend Richard Baxter*. Twenty-three volumes. London, 1830.

Bronkema, Ralph, *The Essence of Puritanism*. Goes, 1929.

Byington, Ezra Hoyt, *The Puritan as Colonist and Reformer*. Boston, 1899.

　　　　　　　　　　The Puritan in England and New England. Third Edition. Boston, 1897.

Chambon, Joseph, *Der Puritanismus, sein Weg von der Reformation bis zum Ende der Stuarts*. Zurich, 1944.

Crouch, Joseph, *Puritanism and Art: An Inquiry into a Popular Fallacy*. London, 1910.

Dark, Sidney, *The Passing of the Puritan*. London, 1946.

Davies, Horton, *The Worship of the English Puritans*. Westminster, 1948.

Flynn, John Stephen, *The Influence of Puritanism on the Political and Religious Thought of the English*. London, 1920.

Frere, Walter Howard, *Puritan Manifestoes, A Study of the Origin of the Puritan Revolt*. New York, 1907.

Garrett, Christina Hallowell, *The Marian Exiles. A Study in the Origins of Elizabethan Puritanism*. Cambridge, 1938.

Haller, William, *The Rise of Puritanism*. New York, 1938.

Hanscom, Elizabeth Deering, *The Heart of the Puritan; Selections from Letters and Journals*. New York, 1917.

Henson, Herbert Hensley, *Puritanism in England*. London, 1912.

Jordan, Wilbur Kitchener, *The Development of Religious Toleration in England.* Four volumes. Cambridge, Massachusetts, 1936–1941.

Knappen, Marshall Mason, *Tudor Puritanism, A Chapter in the History of Idealism.* Chicago, 1939.

Two Elizabethan Puritan Diaries by Richard Rogers and Samuel Ward. Chicago, 1933.

Miller, Perry, *The New England Mind: the Seventeenth Century.* New York, 1939.

Neal, Daniel, *The History of the Puritans . . . from 1517 . . . to 1688.* Revised Edition. Two volumes. New York, 1843–1844.

Nuttall, Geoffrey Fillingham, *The Holy Spirit in Puritan Faith and Experience.* Oxford, 1946.

Parker, Henry, *A Discourse concerning Puritans, Tending to a Vindication.* Second Edition. London, 1641. Ascribed by some to John Ley.

Pearson, Andrew Forret Scott, *Thomas Cartwright and Elizabethan Puritanism.* Cambridge, 1925.

Robertson, Hector Menteith, *Aspects of the Rise of Economic Individualism.* Cambridge, 1935.

Schenk, William, *The Concern for Social Justice in the Puritan Revolution.* London, 1948.

Schneider, Herbert Wallace, *The Puritan Mind.* New York, 1930.

Scholes, Percy Alfred, *The Puritans and Music in England and New England.* London, 1934.

Whiting, Charles Edwin, *Studies in English Puritanism from the Restoration to the Revolution,* 1660–1688. London, 1931.

Wright, Louis Booker, " William Perkins, Elizabethan Apostle of Practical Divinity." *Huntington Library Quarterly,* III, 1940, pp. 171–196.

Chapter II

Baily, Lewes, *The Practice of Piety: Directing a Christian How to Walk that He May Please God.* Amplified by the Author. London, 1669.

Balseng, Paul, *Labadie et le labadisme: étude historique.* Paris, 1908.

Bellardi, Werner, *Die Geschichte der " Christlichen Gemeinschaft " in Strassburg (1546–1550).* Leipzig, 1934.

Beyer-Fröhlich, Marianne, *Empfindsamkeit, Sturm und Drang.* Leipzig, 1936.

Bruns, Hans, *Ein Reformator nach der Reformation. Leben und Wirken Philipp Jakob Speners.* Marburg, 1937.

Bunke, Ernst, *A. H. Francke, der Mann des Glaubens und der Liebe.* Giessen and Basel, 1939.

Burk, Johann Christian Friedrich, *A Memoir of the Life and Writings of John Bengel*. Translated by R. F. Walker. London, 1837.

Directorium der Franckeschen Stiftungen, *Die Stiftungen August Hermann Francke's in Halle*. Halle, 1863.

Franck, Kuno, *A History of German Literature as Determined by Social Forces*. London, 1901.

Francke, August Hermann, *Pietas Hallensis. An Historical Narration* . . . Edinburgh, 1727.

Geissendoerfer, Theodor, *Briefe an August Hermann Francke*. Urbana, Illinois, 1939.

Gloria, Elizabeth, *Der Pietismus als Förderer der Volksbildung*. Zickfeldt, 1933.

Grünberg, Paul, *Philipp Jakob Spener*. Three volumes. Göttingen, 1893.

Heppe, Heinrich, *Geschichte des Pietismus und der Mystik in der reformierten Kirche, namentlich der Niederlande*. Leiden, 1879.

Jüngst-Stetin, Johann, *Pietisten*. Tübingen, 1906.

Kramer, Gustav, *August Hermann Francke: ein Lebensbild*. Two volumes. Halle, 1880–1882.

Lang, August, *Puritanismus und Pietismus. Studien, zu ihrer Entwicklung*. Neukirchen, 1941.

Marholz, Werner, *Der Deutsche Pietismus eine Auswahl von Zeugnissen, Urkunden und Bekenntnissen*. . . . Berlin, 1921.

Mather, Cotton, *Nuncia bona e terra longingua: A Brief Account of Some Good and Great Things A-doing for the Kingdom of God in the midst of Europe*. Boston, 1715. Edited by Kuno Franck in *Americana Germanica* (later *German American Annals*) I, 1897, No. 4, pp. 31-66.

Pinson, Koppel Shub, *Pietism as a Factor in the Rise of German Nationalism*. New York, 1934.

Ritschl, Albrecht, *Geschichte des Pietismus*. Three volumes. Bonn, 1880–1886.

Sachse, Julius Friedrich, *German Pietists of Provincial Pennsylvania*. Philadelphia, 1855.

Sessler, John Jacob, *Communal Pietism Among American Moravians*. New York, 1933.

Spangenberg, August Gottlieb, *The Life of Nicholas Lewis, Count Zinzendorf*. Translated by S. Jackson. London, 1838.

Spener, Philipp Jakob, *Hauptschriften Philipp Jakob Speners*. Edited by Paul Grünberg. Gotha, 1889.

                    Pia Desideria. Edited by Kurt Aland. Berlin, 1940.

CHAPTER III

Balleine, George Reginald, *A History of the Evangelical Party in the Church of England*. London, 1908.

Boston, Thomas, *Human Nature in Its Fourfold State.* . . . Glasgow, 1757.

Cell, George Croft, *The Rediscovery of John Wesley*. New York, 1935.

Coats, Robert Hay, *Types of English Piety*. Edinburgh, 1912.

Cragg, George G., *Grimshaw of Haworth, a Saint in Eighteenth Century Evangelicalism*. London, 1947.

Drummond, Henry, *Dwight L. Moody; Impressions and Facts; with an Introduction by George Adam Smith*. New York, 1900.

Day, Richard Ellsworth, *Bush Aglow: the Life Story of Dwight Lyman Moody*. Philadelphia, 1936.

Davis, Arthur Paul, *Isaac Watts, His Life and Works*. London, 1948.

Doddridge, Philip, *The Rise and Progress of Religion in the Soul*. Philadelphia, 1843.

Elliott-Binns, Leonard Elliott, *The Evangelical Movement in the English Church*. London, 1928.

Fairchild, Hoxie Neale, *Religious Trends in English Poetry*. Vol. II. New York, 1942.

Fisher, Edward, *The Marrow of Modern Divinity*. Edited by C. G. McCrie. Glasgow, 1902.

Gill, Frederick C., *The Romantic Movement and Methodism*. London, 1937.

Hanna, William, *Memoirs of the Life and Writings of Thomas Chalmers*. Edited by James C. Moffat. Four volumes. New York, 1850–1853.

Harrison, Archibald Walter, *The Evangelical Revival and Christian Reunion*. London, 1932.

Howse, Ernest Marshall, *Saints in Politics: the Clapham Sect and Modern Freedom*. Toronto, 1952.

Lee, Umphrey, *The Historical Backgrounds of Early Methodist Enthusiasm*. New York, 1931.

Loane, Marcus L., *Cambridge and the Evangelical Succession*. London, 1952.

Loane, Marcus L., *Oxford and the Evangelical Succession*. London, 1951.

Luccock, Halford Edward; Hutchinson, Paul; and Goodloe, Robert W., *The Story of Methodism*. New York, 1949.

MacArthur, Kathleen, *The Economic Ethics of John Wesley*. New York, 1936.

MacEwen, Alexander Robertson, *The Erskines*. Edinburgh, 1900.

MacInnes, J., *The Evangelical Movement in the Highlands of Scotland, 1688–1800*. Aberdeen, 1951.

McConnell, Francis John, *Evangelicals, Revolutionists and Idealists*. New York, 1942.

Nagler, Arthur Milford, *Pietism and Methodism*. Nashville, 1918.

Poole-Connor, Edward J., *Evangelicalism in England*. London, 1952.

Schrag, Felix James, " Theodorus Jacobus Frelinghuysen." *Church History,* XIV (1945), pp. 201–216.

Scott, Thomas, *The Force of Truth: An Authentic Narrative*. Philadelphia, 1793.

Scougal, Henry, *The Life of God in the Soul of Man*. Edited by W. S. Hudson. Philadelphia, 1948.

Smyth, Charles Hugh Egerton, *Simeon and Church Order*. Cambridge, 1940.

Stevens, Abel, *A History of . . . Methodism*. Three volumes. New York, 1858–1861.

Telford, John, *A Sect that Moved the World*. London, 1907.

Trinterud, Leonard J., *The Forming of an American Tradition. A Reexamination of Colonial Puritanism*. Philadelphia, 1949.

Watt, Hugh, *Thomas Chalmers and the Disruption*. Edinburgh, 1943.

Wesley, John, *The Journal of the Reverend John Wesley*. Edited by Nehemiah Curnock. Eight volumes. London, 1909–1916.

       The Letters of John Wesley. Edited by John Telford. Eight volumes. London, 1931.

       Works of the Reverend John Wesley. Edited by John Emory. Third American Edition. Three volumes. New York, 1835.

Wilberforce, William, *A Practical View of the Prevailing Religious System of Professed Christians. . . .* Second American Edition. Boston, 1799.

Williams, William, *Welsh Calvinistic Methodism. A Historical Sketch*. Second Edition. London, 1884.

CHAPTER IV

Brandreth, Henry Renaud Turner, *The Oecumenical Ideals of the Oxford Movement*. London, 1947.

Brilioth, Yngve Torgny, *The Anglican Revival. Studies in the Oxford Movement*. London, 1925.

Brilioth, Yngve Torgny, *Three Lectures on Evangelicalism and the Oxford Movement*. London, 1934.

Church, Richard William, *The Oxford Movement, Twelve Years, 1833–1845*. London, 1891.

Clarke, Charles Philip Stewart, *The Oxford Movement and After*. London and Oxford, 1932.

Coleridge, Sir John Taylor, *A Memoir of the Reverend John Keble*. Second Edition. New York, 1875.

Dawson, Christopher Henry, *The Spirit of the Oxford Movement*. New York, 1933.

Fairbairn, Andrew Martin, *Catholicism Roman and Anglican*. New York, 1899.

Froude, Richard Hurrell, *Remains of the Late Richard Hurrell Froude*. London, 1838–1839.

Guiney, Louise Imogen, *Hurrell Froude: Memoranda and Comments*. London, 1904.

Harrold, Charles Frederick, *John Henry Newman, An Expository and Critical Study*. . . . London and New York, 1945.

Knox, Edward Arbuthnott, *The Tractarian Movement 1833–1845*. London, 1933.

Liddon, Henry Parry, *Life of Edward Bouverie Pusey*. Four volumes. London and New York, 1893–1897.

May, James Lewis, *The Oxford Movement, Its History and Its Future*. London, 1933.

Middletown, Robert Dudley, *Newman at Oxford; His Religious Development*. New York, 1950.

Newman, John Henry, *Apologia pro vita sua (1864)*. London, 1890.

Ollard, Sidney Leslie, *A Short History of the Oxford Movement*. London and Milwaukee, 1915.

Peck, William George, *The Social Implications of the Oxford Movement*. New York and London, 1933.

Pusey, Edward Bouverie, *Eirenicon*. Three volumes. London, 1865–1870.

Pusey, Edward Bouverie, *Nine Sermons Preached Before the University of Oxford* . . . *1843–1855*. London, 1879.

Russell, George William Erskine, *Dr. Pusey*. London and Oxford, 1912.

Sencourt, Robert (R. E. G. George), *The Life of Newman*. London, 1948.

Shaw, Plato Ernest, *The Early Tractarians and the Eastern Church*. Milwaukee and London, 1930.

Sockman, Ralph W., *The Revival of the Conventual Life in the Church of England in the Nineteenth Century*. New York, 1917.

Stewart, Herbert Leslie, *A Century of Anglo-Catholicism*. New York, 1929.

Taylor, Isaac, *Ancient Christianity and the Doctrines of the Oxford Tracts for the Times*. Two volumes. London, 1839–1842.

Tracts for the Times, by Members of the University of Oxford. Six volumes. London, 1839–1841.

Thureau-Dangin, Paul Marie Pierre, *The English Catholic Revival in the Nineteenth Century* . . . revised and re-edited from a translation by . . . Wilfred Wilberforce. Two volumes. London, 1914.

Walsh, Walter, *The Secret History of the Oxford Movement*. London, 1898.

Ward, Maisie, *Young Mr. Newman*. New York, 1948.

Ward, Wilfred Philip, *The Life of John Henry, Cardinal Newman*. Two volumes. New York and London, 1912.

Ward, Wilfred Philip, *William George Ward and the Oxford Movement*. London, 1889.

Ward, Wilfred Philip, *William George Ward and the Catholic Revival*. London, 1912.

Webb, Clement Charles Julian, *Religious Thought in the Oxford Movement*. London, 1928.

Williams, Thomas Jay, *Priscilla Lydia Sellon*. London, 1950.

CHAPTER V

Bailey, Donald and Marsh, John (Editors), *Intercommunion: the Report of the Theological Commission* . . . *of the World Conference on Faith and Order*. London, 1952.

Batten, Joseph Minton, *John Dury, Advocate of Christian Reunion*. Chicago, 1944.

Bell, George Kennedy Allen, *Christian Unity: the Anglican Position*. London, 1948.

Bell, George Kennedy Allen, *Documents on Christian Unity, 1920–1924,* London, 1924; *Second Series, 1925–1929,* London, 1930; *Third Series, 1930–1948,* London, 1948.

Brandreth, Henry Renaud Turner, *Unity and Reunion, A Bibliography*. London, 1945.

Briggs, Charles Augustus, *Church Unity: Studies of Its Most Important Problems*. New York, 1909.

Brown, Arthur Judson, *Unity and Missions*. New York, 1915.

Brown, William Adams, *Toward a United Church; Three Decades of*

Ecumenical Christianity. Edited by S. M. Cavert. New York, 1946.

Carter, Charles Sydney, *The Reformation and Reunion.* London, 1935.

Douglas, Harlan Paul, *Church Unity Movements in the United States.* New York, 1934.

Fabricius, Cajus, *Corpus Confessionum.* Berlin, 1928.

Flew, R. Newton and Davies, Rupert E., *The Catholicity of Protestantism.* London, 1950.

Florovsky, Georges, *et al., La Sainte Eglise Universelle: confrontation oecuménique.* Neuchâtel and Paris, 1948.

Hodgson, Leonard, *The Ecumenical Movement: Three Lectures. . . .* Sewanee, 1951.

Huntington, William Reed, *The Church Idea; An Essay Toward Unity.* Fourth Edition. New York, 1899.

Marchant, Sir James (Editor), *The Reunion of Christendom.* New York, 1929.

Martin, Hugh (Editor), *Towards Reunion; What the Churches Stand For.* London, 1937.

McNeill, John Thomas, *Unitive Protestantism, a Study in Our Religious Resources.* New York, 1930.

Neill, Stephen Charles, *Christ, His Church and His World.* London, 1948.

Newbigin, James Edward Lesslie, *The Reunion of the Church; A Defence of the South India Scheme.* London, 1948.

Nolde, Otto Frederick, *Toward a World-wide Christianity.* New York, 1946.

Paul, André, *L'unité chrétienne, schismes et rapprochements.* Paris, 1930.

Rouse, Ruth and Neill, Stephen Charles (Editors), *A History of the Ecumenical Movement, 1517–1948.* Philadelphia, 1954.

Sasse, Hermann, *Here We Stand: Nature and Character of the Lutheran Faith,* translated . . . by Theodore G. Tappert. New York, 1938.

Siegmund-Schultze, Friedrich, *Die Einigung der christlichen Kirchen. Sammlung von aussprüchen bedeutender Menchen verschiedener Zeiten.* Basel, 1942.

Siegmund-Schultze, Friedrich (Editor), *Ekklesia. Eine Sammlung von Sellbstdarstellungen der christlichen Kirchen.* Gotha, 1934 — . Projected in ten volumes: incomplete.

Slosser, Gaius Jackson, *Christian Unity, Its History and Challenge.* New York, 1929.

Söderblom, Nathan, *Christian Fellowship.* New York, 1923.

Sperry, Willard Leroyd (Editor), *Religion and Our Divided Denominations*. Cambridge, 1945.

Spinka, Matthew, *John Amos Comenius, That Incomparable Moravian*. Chicago, 1943.

Van Dusen, Henry Pitney, *World Christianity, Yesterday, Today and Tomorrow*. Nashville, 1947.

Visser 't Hooft, Willem Adolph, *Anglo-Catholicism and Orthodoxy: A Protestant View*. London, 1933.

Wedel, Theodore Otto, *The Coming Great Church, Essays on Church Unity*. New York, 1945.

Zander, Leon A., *Vision and Action*. Translated from the Russian by Natalie Doddington. London, 1952.

Chapter VI

Balmes, Jaime Lucio, *Protestantism and Catholicity Compared in Their Effects on the Civilization of Europe*. Written in Spanish and translated from the French. Second Edition. Baltimore, 1851.

Barry, William, *The Coming Age and the Catholic Church. A Forecast*, New York, 1930.

               The Papacy and Modern Times; a Political Sketch, 1303–1870. New York, 1911.

Blanshard, Paul, *American Freedom and Catholic Power*. Boston, 1949.

Bury, John Bagnell, *History of the Papacy in the Nineteenth Century* (1864–1878). London, 1930.

Butler, Dom Cuthbert, *The Vatican Council*. Two volumes. New York, 1930.

Cadoux, Cecil John, *Roman Catholicism and Freedom*. Fourth Edition. London, 1947.

Catechism of the Council of Trent for Parish Priests. Translated with notes by John A. McHugh and Charles J. Callan. New York, 1923.

Coulton, George Gordon, *Papal Infallibility*. London, 1932.

Eckhardt, Carl Conrad, *The Papacy and World-Affairs, Reflected in the Secularization of Politics*. Chicago, 1937.

Fülöp-Miller, René, *Leo XIII and Our Times*. Translated by C. M. R. Bonacina. London, 1937.

Hase, Karl von, *Handbook to the Controversy with Rome*. Translated from the seventh edition by A. W. Stearne. London, 1906.

Jaccard, Frédéric, *Saint Cyran, Précurseur de Pascal*. Lausanne, 1945.

Jalland, Trevor Gervase, *The Church and the Papacy*. London, 1944.

Kidd, Beresford James, *The Counter-Reformation, 1550–1600.* London, 1933.

Lattey, Cuthbert (Editor), *The Papacy. Papers from the School of Catholic Studies, August 7–10, 1923.* Cambridge, 1924.

Leo XIII, Pope, *The Great Encyclical Letters of Pope Leo XIII.* Edited by J. Wynne. Third Edition. New York, 1908.

Liguori, St. Alphonsus Maria, *An Exposition and Defence of the Points of Faith Discussed and Defined by the Sacred Council of Trent.* . . . Translated from the Italian by a Catholic Clergyman. Dublin, 1846.

Manhattan, Avro, *The Catholic Church Against the Twentieth Century.* London, 1947.

Martin, Victor, *Le gallicanisme et la réforme catholique.* Paris, 1919.

McKnight, John P., *The Papacy: a New Appraisal.* New York, 1952.

Nielsen, Fredrik Kristian, *The History of the Papacy in the XIXth Century.* Translated under the direction of A. J. Mason. New York, 1906.

Nippold, Friedrich, *The Church in the Nineteenth Century.* Translated by L. H. Schwab. New York, 1900.

Schaff, Philip, *Creeds of Christendom.* Three volumes. Fourth Edition. New York, 1919.

Schmidt, Kurt Dietrich, *Studien zur Geschichte des Konzils von Trient.* Tübingen, 1925.

Smith, George D., *et al., The Teaching of the Catholic Church.* Two volumes. London, 1948.

Wallace, Lillian Parker, *The Papacy and European Diplomacy, 1869–1878.* Chapel Hill, 1948.

Rome and the Study of Scripture: a Collection of Papal Enactments. Fourth Edition. St. Meinard, Indiana, 1946.

INDEX